Your Kids Their Future

Every Parent's Guide to Helping Your Child Become Employable

by
Gary R. Morrison

Landon Solutions
Waynesboro, Virginia

©1999 by Gary R. Morrison
All Rights Reserved.
Landon Solutions, Waynesboro, Virginia

Printed by Closson Press in the United States of America
First Printing February 1999

Library of Congress Cataloging in Publication Data

Morrison, Gary R.
Your Kids Their Future

1. Education
2. Parenting
3. Self-help
I. Title

Library of Congress Catalog Card Number: 98-91256

ISBN 0-9662651-0-6

special thanks to:

Art Burgamasco,
a master motivator

Jack McCartan,
a master educator

Ted Maroney,
a rebuilder

also,
Calvin Clark
Tom McAraw
Mary Del Brady
Richard Morrison
MEO
Colonel Edward B. Young
Doris Brown
Mary Sue McAllister
Elizabeth Gogniat
John Trumbetta
and
The U.S. Department of Labor

Most importantly....
thanks to my wife,
Susan
for your support and encouragement.

CONTENTS

PREFACE

All parents want their children to have a better life than they had, and all parents spend a majority of their adult life making sure that this is the case. In fact, there is nothing that parents will not sacrifice to ensure their children's happiness and success.

Many parents, however, have found that when it comes to helping their children make decisions about what to do after high school, they are unprepared. The answers used to be simple. If you worked in a town with a mill or a factory, your child went down, filled out an application, got hired, and lived happily ever after. If your child was academically inclined, you sent your child to college. If your child was academically inclined, and you didn't have a mill or factory nearby, you sent them to the military. Simple.

Things have changed. The opportunities to acquire gainful employment directly from high school have virtually disappeared. The military has become a great deal more specialized and selective. And, a four year degree is no longer the ticket to success that it once was.

These changes have not been entirely gradual. In fact, the changes have happened so fast that even those who specialize in educating and counseling your children have had trouble keeping up with those changes. If these people have trouble keeping up with the changes, where does this leave the parents?

With all of these changes it is no wonder that there are so many people who are highly educated and yet highly unemployable. Young people who took out loans to attend colleges and schools can't pay back those loans. Some are having to return to education or training just to keep the jobs they have. And more children than ever before are moving back home with their parents because they just can't afford to live alone.

The "empty nest syndrome" has turned into the "overcrowded nest syndrome". The agony of too many adults in

1

one home has become a modern day symptom of an over-educated, under-employable young population.   The golden years of retirement, travel, and free time have turned into the years when babysitting grandchildren is the daily activity.   Grown children living at home, sometimes with their entire new family, have created incredible stresses on relationships.

All of this is happening when, strangely enough, American companies are hiring from overseas. Some of this country's best entry-level jobs are going to imported employees while American children struggle to live independently on low-level positions.

So, what is the solution?   Well, you're already a part of the solution. You are educating yourself and becoming armed with the information you will need to prevent this from becoming your problem. This is what parents need to do in order to be able to continue their sacrifice for their children.

Parents need to be at the center of this solution because there is no one else who has as great a stake in seeing a solution to this problem. No company, teacher, or counselor has as much of an interest in your child's success as you.   And, unfortunately, even the children who will be so affected by this solution don't have the insight to effectively overcome this challenge alone.

The responsibility for preparing children for the world of work lies solely on the shoulders of the parent. Parents who are informed and prepared will reap the rewards of their children's successes, and the rewards are many.   Pride, happiness, and FREEDOM lie ahead for those parents who correctly assist their children explore, select, train, and then excel in the career of their choice. I hope this book will help. Good luck!

INTRODUCTION

Before we begin I would like to take some time to explain who I am, where I come from, and why it is that I thought it was important to write about the subject of career planning. This is not necessary for you to know this in order to use the information in this book, but I think that it will help you see why this book was written. Keep in mind that this book was written for parents, but can also be helpful to any person who finds him/herself in a position of giving career advice to students who are about to leave high school.

I chose to direct this information primarily to parents for very personal reasons. The first reason goes back to when I was a teenager and thinking about what I would do after I graduated from high school.

Like most high school students my head was filled with dreams. I couldn't wait to shed the shackles of education, get my own place, and start living life MY way. Many afternoons were wasted away thinking and talking about how great it would be.

Also, like many high school students, my career choices changed from day to day. First, I was going to be a professional football player, then a doctor, then an actor, then a soldier....and on and on. My enthusiasm for the future was shared by most of my peers, and we grew more excited with every discussion on the subject.

As my senior year came closer, however, that enthusiasm began to change to fear. It became apparent that I really didn't know what it was that I wanted to do after high school. And, even if I could settle on one career, I still didn't know what I would have to do in order to get there. This, compounded with the pressure of having to make this decision soon, made what should have been a time of hope and happiness into a time of doubt and anxiety. Being the red-blooded teenager that I was, I did the only thing that seemed to make sense...I played my stereo even louder. (My 8-tracks of LED ZEPPELIN always did the job!)

It became apparent that this was not a decision that could be handled alone, and I began to seek advice.

The first person I turned to was my guidance counselor. He was a great guy who had dedicated himself to helping students. Although his desk seemed to buckle under the weight of piles of paperwork, he was always able to make time for every student and every crisis even if it meant dragging those piles of paper home with him in his beat-up old Volvo. "He had to have the answers," I thought. His walls were lined with shelves of catalogs from every school imaginable. He had seen thousands of students graduate and become successful. "Surely he would be the man with the plan."

I can still see him appearing from behind his paper fortress with his broad smile and hand extended. (That was one of the things we liked about him. He always shook our hands and treated us like adults.) We sat and talked about football for a while before getting to the real reason that I had come to see him. After listening to me explain my dilemma, he asked the most difficult question that I had ever been asked -- even more difficult than any question on the SAT test, "Well, what to you want to be?"

I then went to my teachers. They were like many teachers these days. Although they were hired to teach a specific subject, on which they had received years of training, their roles were significantly expanded beyond their expertise. The roles of coach, counselor, cop, crisis intervention worker, mentor, role model, and friend were quickly added to their job description after they had signed their contracts. Most accepted these new roles gladly and did their best to provide us with as much help as possible. When answering my question, many of them would rely on a very important part of the puzzle-- what subjects I did well in at school. The problem was that they would recommend that I continue to study that subject after high school. This still left me with the question,"What do I want to be?"

My next option was to turn to my parents. This created quite a dilemma. After all, I had just spent the last few years convincing myself that my parents didn't know anything, and here I was turning to them for advice. "OK", I was forced to admit, "Perhaps they know a little about something. They had lived to be really old and couldn't have done that without acquiring some wisdom."

They had been as close to perfect parents as you will ever find. My brother and I grew up without a care. Our memories of childhood were filled with good memories. They were tough on us when we needed it and didn't spoil us or let us run wild, but they did everything in their power to provide for us and keep us healthy and happy.

Our old home movies tell the story well. As I have matured I have begun to notice things that before went undetected. As you watch my brother and me do the things that kids do, in the background you can see the cars my parents drove, nothing fancy and plenty of primer. Their clothes were often well worn. The living room furniture, usually second had stuff, begged for replacement. These people, I have grown to appreciate, had sacrificed all of their married lives... for us.

There was nothing that they wouldn't do for my brother and me. But with this question, "What should I do after high school?" I had finally placed them in a position where they felt they couldn't help me. As you could probably tell from my father's powerful, crooked hands, he had worked in the mill most of his adult life. That was the only life he knew. He could have easily set me up with a job there, but again being a parent, he wanted me to have a better life. My mother had done so many jobs that she couldn't even remember them all. Aside from a short career as a freelance reporter, they were survival jobs, many of them unpleasant and very unfulfilling. These were the kind of jobs that she did to help pay the bills and carry us through hard times, and not the kind of stuff she wanted for her kid.

I do remember their asking me one question in particular. It was a question that affirmed my fear that teachers, parents, and guidance counselors were all part of a big conspiracy. They asked, "Well, what do you want to be?"

5

I chose to follow the advice of one of my teachers, and I went off to college to study one of my favorite subjects, Biology. I had no idea what I would do with my training, but I did know that Biology was my favorite subject and would eventually lead somewhere. This teacher did say one thing that would be particularly significant. He said that even if I decided later that I didn't like Biology, I wouldn't be alone. He then added that many students don't end up working in the field for which they prepare.

I finished four grueling years, got my bachelors degree, and began my career search. Now that I had put off my decision long enough I was once again forced to deal with that old nagging question, "So, what do I want to be?"

I could not believe it. Here I was, four years out of high school, educated, deep in debt, and I still had no clue what I wanted to be. Sure, I checked around to see just what was out there, but nothing that related to my major interested me. There were some jobs that I could do where you needed a degree (any degree) to get hired, but these were not nearly what I wanted to do. And those jobs that seemed interesting just did not pay enough for me to live independently while paying back my student loans. "This was not the way it was supposed to be," I thought.

For two years I bounced around in the job market. These jobs were a means to make a little (and I mean a little) money, but they were hardly positions in which I could see myself building a life-long career.

My big break came when I stumbled across a friend who was going to teach at the same military school from which we had both graduated. He told me that there was an opening for a Biology teacher, and that I should apply. I did, and was hired. I was very lucky because this school allowed me to get my teaching credentials (something that I did not have) while I taught.

So, there I was, a Biology teacher (a thought that scared even me). I did everything I could to be a good teacher and after the fact began taking courses on how to do this "teaching thing". I honestly think that I was a fairly good teacher even though much of

6

the time I felt like I was "winging it". I also began to assume all of those extra responsibilities, that like teaching, I was never really trained for.

The most difficult thing for me to do was give advice to my students about career planning. They seemed to believe that being a teacher you should have all the answers. Obviously, I didn't, but the one answer I had the most difficulty helping them answer was the one that I still had not answered for myself, " So, what do you think I should be?"

I taught at this high school for five years, and loved every minute of it. I have to admit there are few careers with the emotional reward of teaching. But, after a few years, it occurred to me that this was not something that I wanted to do for the rest of my life.

The next step for me was to take a position as a Career Development Specialist for the Pittsburgh Technical Institute. At first my responsibilities were nothing more than those of a recruiter. The most enjoyable part of this job was that I was given the opportunity to do public speaking every day throughout the school year. This is something that I loved doing in high school, but never knew could have career possibilities.

As part of my continuing education at PTI, I was required to attend training sessions, read literature on careers, become familiar with what was needed by employers, and to stay abreast of anything that was hot regarding employment issues. Because of the knowledge I was gaining, I soon became a very valuable resource for many organizations. I soon found myself speaking to civic groups, teachers groups, trade organizations, military personnel, and parents. There was such a demand for this information, that I was sometimes overwhelmed.

One other interesting thing happened to me while working at the Pittsburgh Technical Institute. When a student signed up to go to school at PTI, they weren't permitted to pick and choose subjects - they had to pick a career. Before starting their first class at PTI, they knew exactly which career they would be training for. This was an approach that was not unique to career schools but was used with all of the six fields for which this school trained.

While helping place these students in the job market, it dawned on me what an incredible advantage they had -- they had already picked and received the required training for a specific career. This made me think about the people that I went to school with who had done the same thing before entering colleges or other forms of career training. Small as that number may have been, these people had done it the right way and avoided the hassles and heartbreak that the rest of us had endured.

As you will see later this is a very important part of the advice that I now give to parents. Looking at my own personal career history and comparing it to what I was seeing with these students graduating from this school illustrated to me that I would have benefited greatly from such a focused approach.

A key factor that motivated me to write this book came one afternoon when my parents were over to visit. My father knew I had a big mouth but couldn't quite understand how it was that I made a living running it. He asked me if he could sit down and watch one of the video tapes that I had made while speaking on the subject of careers. He watched intently for forty-five minutes as I presented the career planning information that makes up much of this book. When it was over, he turned to me and in an apologetic tone said, "Gary, I wish I would have known this when you were in high school". There was no need for an apology-- BUT, it occurred to me that there must be countless other parents who felt this way as well.

And so you have it - the reason for this book - so that no parent would have to be faced with the frustration of not being able to help their child with one of life's most significant decisions.

This question, "What do you want to be?" was the one question that I could never answer. And, even if I could answer it, I still wouldn't have known how to get there.

Seeing kids and parents struggling with this decision even now, and remembering the difficulty that I had with that same decision has brought me to the premise of this book. If you can help your child to answer this question and can also to show them the ways to reach their particular career goals, you will be giving them a tremendous boost toward a successful future. You will also free yourself of the feeling of despair that comes with not being able to help your child through this most difficult decision.

This book is designed for parents to be used as a guide. It is user friendly and practical with step by step instructions that should help you as much as it helps your child. Let's get started.

PARENT TO PARENT

"It seems like just yesterday that I was sitting on my favorite chair having a discussion with my sons about the future. Being only thirteen months apart in age, it seemed appropriate to talk about many things to both of them at the same time. Sean, the oldest, was at one end of the couch while Mike laid at the opposite end. Mike had fallen asleep. How rewarding it was to have Sean's undivided attention. The excitement twinkled in his eyes as he listened to every word. His face glowed with the smiles that came from each career suggestion. He laughed about being an astronaut. He shared a distant stare at the mention of being a doctor. The sirens at the fire hall startled both boys but lead to a discussion of the thrills of fire fighting. Perhaps teaching would be a great choice as a way to follow in their parent's footsteps. The list went on and on. I finally knew he had heard enough when his head drifted back, his hands and feet stopped moving, and the pacifier dropped from his mouth. Oh, how proud I felt, knowing that they would some day be the best at whatever they chose to do. I believed it every bit as much as their mom did."

WHERE TO BEGIN?

CAREER EXPLORATION

Every great journey begins with a first simple step. Helping children reach their career potential begins the same way. There will be miles of roads and countless intersections, but until that first step is taken there can be no growth, learning, or progress. Parents and children are quite often confused as to what should be that first step. The first section of this book is designed to give parents enough guidance so that taking that first step with their children will be easy and can be taken with confidence.

GETTING STARTED

The first thing that you will need to do in the process of helping your child to become employable is to encourage him/her to explore some career goals. By career goals I mean the kinds of jobs that your child may want to do for a living when he/she is finally done with his/her education or training. With most young people this is a wide open process. They may be familiar with only a few careers. Those careers will usually be limited to the ones they see glamorized on television as well as the careers of their parents, teachers, and friends. This first step is designed to open your child's eyes to as many possibilities as possible.

WHEN TO BEGIN

It is best if your child can explore careers that might interest them as early in high school as possible. By the end of your child's junior year in high school, your child will need to have been exposed to as many careers as possible and know enough about these careers that he/she can select the one career that he/she will pursue. The reason your child needs to do this so early is that his/her senior year will be spent exploring, selecting, and applying for colleges or other training programs.

ANSWERING THE QUESTION WHY

The benefits to your child of having clear-cut career goals when preparing for their post-high school years will become more obvious as we proceed through this book. It is extremely important in the process of helping your child become employable, but there are even more benefits.

Anyone who has spent any time around children knows that when they reach those teenage years, everything has to be justified. Gone are the days of just saying that the reason they should do something is because "I said so", or "because it's good for you". Teenagers need to know "why" if they are expected to follow advice, parental wishes, or even rules. Sure, you can

14

crack down and make your teenager do things, but that becomes less effective and more unpleasant as they get older.

Parents of self-motivated, goal-oriented children are truly blessed. These kids rarely ask "why" ... because they have their own answers. They have a reason to do things right. They have their own reason to do well in school, to stay out of trouble, and to do all those other things their parents want them to do, but don't have to tell them to do.

Having your child select a career goal, and get excited about that career goal, gives them an answer to their own question, "why". Most careers worth having will have requirements that are very similar to your own wishes and rules-good grades...good conduct...etc.. Don't be surprised if your child becomes more motivated, agreeable, and positive once he/she has explored and then selected his/her own future. I am a firm believer that the worst thing for teenagers, and one of the main reasons for much of the trouble they experience today, is due to a lack of direction. Teenagers and limbo are a dangerous mix. Getting teenagers involved at an earlier age with selecting their own paths can help to solve many more problems than just employability.

ADVICE FOR BEGINNING

There are a few things that you need to consider as you go through this process. Read all of the information about career exploration before you sit down with your child and begin. Thoroughly understanding this information will help you to avoid some of the mistakes that parents have told me they have made with their children, and will also help prepare you to overcome any objections or concerns that your child may come up with along the way. On occasion you may wish to refer back to some of these suggestions to refresh your memory. Some of these suggestions will seem to make more sense after you have begun.

GO WINDOW SHOPPING

When speaking to parents and children about how to approach the first steps of career exploration, I often compare it to "window shopping". Think back to the last time you had to buy a gift for someone, but did not know what to buy. Many of you who find yourselves in this situation will begin a process of "window shopping". You get in the car and go to the local mall or shopping center and begin to shop around. Traveling from store to store you browse the shelves looking at all of your options. At some point in this process you might come up with a "short list" of ideas that might be the right gift. You may even stumble across that one gift that jumps out at you and seems to say, "This is it!"

This approach usually proves to be successful, because ideas that would have never come to mind, if you did not "shop around", now present themselves. There is no way you can come up with that ideal gift by just sitting in the house thinking. You have to know what is out there. And the only way to do that is to get out and explore.

This is exactly the approach that I suggest when exploring careers. This part of the process is designed to allow kids to "shop around" in the job market. And, just as is when you shop for that perfect gift, your child will develop a "short list" of possible careers or even stumble across that one career that will be perfect.

PICK SPECIFIC CAREERS

It is very important that the choices made by your son or daughter are narrowed down to specific careers. In order to be employable, your child will need to approach an employer and tell that employer exactly who he/she is and what he/she can do. The days are gone when you can get a job just because you are "a people person who has a strong desire to be successful".

It is a good idea to start with a field, but the result that you are looking for, and will eventually work with, must be a specific career within that field. For example, your child may say that he/she wants to work in the medical field, but he/she needs to be encouraged to come up with something specific within that field -- a nurse, a respiratory technician, a doctor. The true test for this would be to take their choice and put in this sentence - In five, six, or seven years I will be a _____. If your child's choice fits into this sentence, then you have done this part of the process correctly.

Be prepared to reassure your child that you are only looking at possibilities, and that he/she can abandon any particular career at any time during this process if it becomes apparent that this particular career might not be what he/she wants to do. This part of the process is just exploratory, and no one is asking for any commitments... yet. (Important note -- If your child picks a career such as a doctor, a lawyer, the kind of career that you already know will take longer than the five, six, or seven year period that we are using, his/her sentence will look more like, "In five years I will be in Medical school or in Law school", etc.. There are also other special considerations for these students that we will cover later when referring to graduate school, law school, and medical school.)

PICK SEVERAL CAREERS

Because this part of the process is exploratory, it is encouraged that you allow your child to select several careers. Encourage him/her to pick more than one career, but on each attempt at this process, limit the choices to a manageable number. A good suggestion would be around five. And these five careers would be the five most interesting careers at this time. As you work with your child, some or maybe even all of these career possibilities may be abandoned. If this happens, simply replace the abandoned career with a new choice. What you will see in the long run will be a "process of elimination" that will lead you to a specific career goal.

STAY POSITIVE

This process of choosing careers to explore can be extremely frustrating for both the parent and the child. It will be up to you as the parent to keep the process a positive and fun exercise. Avoid discouraging your child from exploring a certain career. If you think that it might be a dead-end road, explore it anyway. If there is no future in that particular career, let your child find out for him/herself. You might also encounter situations where your child picks something that you think is unrealistic or impractical. If this is the case, continue to encourage them, but work backwards towards a career goal that is related to his/her choice, but is more reachable. Remember that the purpose of this exercise is for your child to find a career that excite him or her. If your child picks a career because he/she thinks you want them to go in a certain direction, your child will eventually loose enthusiasm, and the whole process will be a wash.

STAY "REWARD" NOT "CONSEQUENCE" ORIENTED

A common mistake that we all make when dealing with teenagers is focusing on the negative consequences of their actions. We can all remember a time when we told a young person that, if they kept doing what they were doing, they "will wind up flipping burgers for the rest of their lives". While kids need to be warned about the dangers that might lie ahead, focusing on the negative consequences without throwing in the positive rewards can be dangerous.

One of the major problems with pointing out these negative consequences is that we force kids to visualize themselves in this negative situation. Every time we say to a kid "you're gonna find yourself flipping burgers if you don't do better", we force that child to see themselves in that position. We also reinforce the fears that they won't succeed.

A better approach is to consistently remind them of the rewards of positive behavior and choices. Saying something like, "Keep those grades up and play your cards right, and you'll be

driving a Porsche and living in a mansion! I can see it happening"
A far better image than the former.

LET YOUR CHILD KNOW THAT THE CAREER HE/SHE FINALLY SELECTS WILL BE HIS/HER FIRST CAREER

One of the things that has made this decision so difficult for children in the past is that they are overwhelmed by the idea that the career that they are selecting is one that they will have to do for the rest of their lives. This is simply not the case. It is now projected that the average person will change careers from seven to eight times during their adult life. This fact can be used to relieve some of the pressure. Explain this to your child, and make sure that he/she understands that the first career selected will simply be a starting point. Your child will most likely, after working in that field for several years, find other opportunities that will lead him/her in directions you never could predict at this point in their lives. Again, this first career goal that you will end up with after your exploration, although very specific, will be just a starting point.

USING RESOURCE MATERIALS AND ORGANIZATIONS

There are countless careers out there, and most people cannot possibly be aware of all of them. Somewhere in that cluster of careers, however, is the one career that will "light the fire" of your child, and be the one that he/she will select and run with.

Finding out what these careers are is much easier than most people think. I suggest two main sources, one of which is within reach at this very moment.

1) The Sunday Paper

The most obvious and accessible source of career information is the Sunday paper. If you do not already have a subscription, get one. You will only need the Sunday or Saturday edition, because these are usually the ones that will have the largest "help-wanted" sections. Make sure that the paper comes from the largest metropolitan paper in you area. Small town, local papers often have a limited number of career listings. If you live between more than one large metro area, consider getting papers from both cities.

There are advantages and disadvantages to using the Sunday paper. Lets look at the advantages first.

> The careers that are listed in the ads are obviously in demand at the moment. This is something that always has to be considered. There is no use picking a career to train for if there is no demand for that career. If companies are asking for certain specialties in the paper, then these specialties are obviously in demand. You will immediately notice the size of certain fields. Compare, for example, the section for computer and medical professionals to sections dedicated to other fields.

> These are the careers that are in demand in your area. Something to consider, especially if your child likes the area where you live and would like to stay near family and friends. Teenagers will many times talk a good game about wanting to see

the world, but when it comes down to leaving behind friends, girlfriends, boyfriends, and family sometimes their bark is worse than their bite. At the end of this book you will find a chapter that lists local employment centers. You may wish to contact someone in your hometown if your child does indeed want to stay in the area.

> What you will see in the paper are specific positions. In many cases, they will also spell out exactly the kind of education that is required -- a tremendous advantage when you begin picking training options.

> In many cases the ad will give the salary for that particular position -- an important factor to consider.

There are also some disadvantages. You will soon see why I recommend the newspaper as only a supplemental source.

The disadvantages:

> The newspaper will only have a small sample of what is actually out there. The jobs in the paper, as we have already indicated, represent only local needs. Also, only about a fourth of the positions currently available in your area will be advertised in the paper.

> These job descriptions and responsibilities for the listed position will be very short and incomplete. It would be hard for most people to truly understand what you would really be doing on a day-to-day basis.

> What you will see in the paper is what is in demand right now and not necessarily in the future.

As you can see, there are some definite advantages to using the newspaper as one of your sources. You should definitely use it, but keep in mind that it does have its limitations and should be used as a supplemental source.

Have your child go through the paper with you every

21

weekend, and if something strikes him/her as interesting cut the ad out and keep it handy. Since the descriptions will be incomplete you will need to find out more about what this career is all about. The best source for this information is the second method that I will recommend for finding careers.

2) The Occupational Outlook Handbook

The second resource is probably *the most important source of information that you can have in your possession* as you help your child through this process. It is so important that I recommend to all parents I speak with that they purchase one for their home. The book is called THE OCCUPATIONAL OUTLOOK HANDBOOK. (I will be referring to this throughout the book as "OOH"). This book is put out annually by the U.S. Department of Labor and details almost every career that you can imagine. And, not only are careers listed, but they also describe in detail the nature of the work, the working conditions, who the employers are, the training required, the job outlook, and earnings.

There is also a section in the beginning of the book about anticipated trends in the job market. The information in this book is absolutely invaluable. If you don't yet have this book, *GET IT.* You can find it at larger book stores in the employment section or you can order it from the US Department of Labor. Here is the address.

Bureau of Labor Statistics
Publications Sales Center
P.O. Box 2145
Chicago, IL 60690

For information or to order with a credit card call
(312) 353-1880.

They also have a site on the web -
www.bls.gov/ocohome.htm

The site can be very helpful, but I still suggest purchasing the book. Having it lie on the coffee table makes it far more

22

accessible, and prevents the distractions of the web.

Don't allow yourself to procrastinate. I just can't emphasize enough how valuable this will be for you. Most of the parents that I have introduced to this book were absolutely amazed.

When you scan through the book you will see that it is divided into career field sections. Have your child find a field that interests him/her. Then have him/her go through the section dedicated to that field and pick out the career or careers that look interesting. You can also locate the careers that your child has found in the paper to get a complete description of what someone in that particular position does. If that description matches the interests of your child, then you have one of the five careers with which you will start. Simply use the appendix to find the career that interests your child. You will usually find one to two pages on any career you wish to learn about.

Remember to focus on the career and not on how you get trained for that career. As we have said before, we will deal with this later. To get involved with this at the beginning of the procedure would simply make things too confusing. Your child will sometimes have the tendency to get ahead of the game and pick careers based simply on how he/she will get there. It will be up to you to assure them that you will cross that bridge when you come to it.

These are the two quickest and most practical methods that parents can use to help their children explore career options from home. The following is a brief description on some other approaches.

3) Check with local companies

There is really no more direct approach that this. What you will be required to do is contact some of the local companies in your area and ask them what specialties are in demand. In some cases which companies to contact will be obvious. For example, if you have a child that is interested in the medical field, you would first need to call someone at your local hospital. If your child has an interest in cars, you might wish to contact local dealerships, garages, or automobile manufacturing plants.

After finding someone in the personnel department or public relations department that would be willing to give you five minutes, just explain why you are calling and ask them what positions are in the highest demand. You might also ask which of these professions will stay in demand and which have too many people applying for them.

When you find something that interests your child, you might then contact someone in the department that hires this kind of person directly to ask specific questions about job opportunities that exist at that facility.   Also ask about pay, advantages, hours, and other positives and negatives of the job. If the position still seems to be something that your son or daughter would like, you might then ask if your child could come in and spend a half of a day observing them on the job. There really is no better way to learn than by being there.

If you feel uncomfortable about searching for, contacting, and arranging this on your own, contact your child's guidance counselor. As part of the School to Work Initiative, recently enacted in many public schools, there is a program called "Job Shadowing". Your school may already have agreements with local employers to allow students to visit the workplace and observe different careers in action.

4) Help your local school organize a CAREER fair

You may wish to contact your local PTA or school officials and suggest, or help to organize a career fair. Most schools these days have college fairs where they invite colleges, career schools, and the military to come in and visit in a cafeteria or gymnasium. These are great sources of information on how to get trained for different careers, but not necessarily on the careers themselves. As I have explained before, this is putting the cart before the horse.   Before you choose your path you have to know your destination.   Another drawback of this is that the people who represent these schools have obviously not done all of the careers that their school trains for and really cannot be expert sources on the complexities of these various positions. They are also "salespeople" responsible for doing whatever it takes to get your child to pick their program.

The kind of career fair that I am talking about is one that puts an emphasis on the career. The ideal situation would be where you have people from various career fields come in and set-up in the cafeteria. They could sit at tables labeled with their position -- physician, mechanic, hairdresser, programmer, accountant, etc. This way, students and their parents can walk from table to table and speak briefly with individuals in the career fields that interest them.

This form of career fair gives a tremendous advantage to students because they are able to explore so many options in one short period of time. It is also very valuable to be able to talk directly with a person who is where your child wants to be. The drawback is that this sort of event is a logistical nightmare, and not something that any one person could successfully organize alone. Organizing something like this would require very enthusiastic, dedicated people, and the cooperation of school officials, parents, community leaders, and local employers. I have seen it done. If you think its a good idea, get with some other parents and present the idea to your local PTA, local principle, or school board. And...be prepared to volunteer.

5) Contact your Child's Favorite Teachers.

Every student will have a favorite subject while he/she is in high school. In many cases the teachers that specialize in that subject will also be your child's favorite teachers. Contact those teachers directly and ask them what careers are available that relate to the specific subject that they teach.

Don't hesitate to call. Most of the thousands of teachers with whom I have been familiar are extremely dedicated educators. The reason they got into education in the first place was the reward of helping kids, and this would be just one more opportunity to do what they have dedicated their professional lives to. They will also, in many cases, know your child very well and will be able to give you a different perspective on your child's abilities and interests.

6) Check with your local Boy Scout office.

The Boy Scouts of America have a group called the Explorer program. This program has various posts, and many of these posts are dedicated to career exploration. The meetings are sponsored by local companies, schools, churches, and civic organizations. In a casual, club-like setting your child will have the opportunity to participate in career related activities with other children who have similar career interests. There are no uniforms to be worn, and the dues are minimal. This is an ideal way to explore careers especially if your child is beginning this process early in his/her high school years.

7) Consider your local Vocational-Technical School.

As you begin this process, get some information from your local Vocational Technical School on what career training they offer. These schools have become extremely diversified and offer a broad range of career related education and training from which your child can benefit while still getting his/her high school diploma. Most people see these schools as only a way to train for certain careers, but they can also be used as a way to explore certain careers. If any of the careers that interest your child are taught at one of these schools, you may wish to consider speaking with a representative from that school.

8) Have your child take the *ASVAB Career Exploration Program.*

The U.S. Armed Forces has a program that tests students to determine what careers might be in their future. Students who are a part of this program will take an aptitude battery (ASVAB), complete an interest survey, and will complete "work values" exercises. This is a great program to increase career, as well as self, awareness. Contact your local guidance counselor or

military recruiter for more information.

THINGS TO ASK AS YOUR CHILD EXPLORES CAREER CHOICES

Now that you know where to look for careers, as well as information on those careers, you will need to know what to ask. The following list of questions should be proposed to your child as you examine each career.

1.) Is this career choice something that you will enjoy?

The answer to this question is extremely important. The career that your child selects will occupy a larger chunk of his/her adult life than any other activity. He/she can expect to spend, at very least, eight to ten hours out of every working day in his/her chosen profession. The American work-week has steadily grown longer. And, as anyone who has ever had a lousy job can tell you, if you don't enjoy your job, you won't enjoy your life.

As you find out what your child will be doing in his/her chosen career, compare that to what he/she already enjoys. Are there any similarities to what he/she enjoys doing in his/her spare time? Is this career related to a subject that he/she enjoyed while in school? Are the kind of people that he/she will be working with be the kind that he/she enjoys spending time with? Will he/she enjoy the physical surroundings where this career will take him/her?

The idea of enjoying a career is very subjective. For example, how many of you would enjoy a career that would require you to shovel horse manure all day? Very few, right? Now, how many of you could learn to enjoy shoveling horse manure if that particular career paid $100 per hour? Ah-ha! This is a whole different story. In fact, if it was common knowledge what "Horse Manure Engineers" were paid, this position could be one of great prestige.

I can see it now -- a party discussion between two eligible bachelorettes: "That's John, he's new in my apartment complex." "Really, what does he do?" "Well, rumor has it he is in manure!"

28

" Wow, what a catch!"

The idea of enjoying your job should be replaced by "job satisfaction". "Job satisfaction" is more appropriate because it implies that the person doing a certain job is getting what he/she wants from that job. Every person wants something different from what they do for a living. It may be financial rewards, a sense of importance, a chance to help people, or even the opportunity to pursue a passion. In most cases it will be a combination of all of the above, with an emphasis on one or two of these reasons.

2.) Is the income level acceptable?

Think back to the OOH as well as what people in the field have told you. Keep in mind that young people sometimes have trouble knowing what would be acceptable. Many kids see the salaries paid to professional athletes and think that they will make something in that range. I have, on many occasions while teaching and speaking, shared with students my salary range. In many instances, despite the fact that I think I'm doing OK, I have been slapped with the response, "Dude, is that all?" As demoralizing as this can be, it has proven to me, time and time again, how unrealistic the income expectations of teenagers are.

To help your children with this, you may wish to share with them your own salary history, including your current income. Also share with them your current expenses, so that they will thoroughly understand what income level is required to live the way you live now. Follow this by having them write their own "standard of living expectations". Start by listing expenses for your child's housing arrangements including bills. Follow this by what kind of car they would like to drive and approximate the payments of such a vehicle. Include clothing allowances, insurance payments, food budgets, and spending-cash. This practical exercise can be very valuable for grounding your child's income expectations in reality.

3.) Are people in this particular career in demand?

One of the biggest mistakes that people have made in the past is training for something that is not in demand. Your child can train to be the best "widget maker" in the world, but if the world doesn't need widgets...he/she will be an unemployed "widget maker".

If you are not sure about the demand check back to the OOH. For each career there should be an entry about the number of positions available as well as whether or not that career field will be growing. If the source for particular career information was a local employer, ask the employer if there will still be a demand in the next few years?

OTHER TIPS

START A "CAREERS TO EXPLORE" FOLDER

Keep a folder handy so that your search will be organized. Start your folder by including five sheets of paper, one sheet for each career. At the top of each sheet, put the title of the career and use the rest of the sheet to take notes. Your notes should include things like...salary... are these people in demand?...will I have to relocate to do this job?...what do these people do that I like?...what do these people do that I might not like?

MAKE THIS PROCESS A CENTER OF FAMILY LIFE

This process is not something that should be shelved and brought up only on occasion. Make it a part of your daily life. Post a sheet of paper on the refrigerator with a list of things that "have been done" as well as a list of things "to be done".

Give yourself deadlines. Because our lives are so hectic, something like this can easily be put off till tomorrow. Every day that is put off will make it more difficult to get back on track.

Discuss at what point you are in the process every day. Leave the Occupational Outlook Handbook out and clearly visible in the living room.

Use the arrival of the Sunday paper as an opportunity to go over together what is in the employment section.

START YOUR "TO DO" LIST NOW.

To do:
Call newspaper for Sunday subscription
Call bookstore for Occupational Outlook Handbook
          or write to U.S. Dept. of Labor
Call high school Principal, Guidance Counselor, or PTA about career fair
Call Personnel Director of at least one local company
Favorite subject_____ --Find related Careers
Check Explorer program
Get information from local Vocational-Technical school
etc..

TIME TO GET STARTED

It is now time to get this show on the road. Don't do any of the things beyond career exploration until your child has selected about five careers. Everything that needs to be done later will be made much easier when your child has explored and then selected his/her specific career goals. The following section contains a list and very brief description of what could be called the "25 strongest career fields". Use it as a guide to what is stable as well as an example of what your career exploration sheets should look like.

If you have not yet done so, ask your son or daughter if he/she has put any thought into what he/she wants to do after high school. (If he/she has not, then ask him/her what his/her dream job would be.) Whatever you do, please, share in his/her excitement. Let the discussion begin, and tell him/her what you have been reading.

Have confidence in the fact that you are now far better prepared than most parents that have done this in the past. Your confidence will transfer to your child and give you a tremendous boost towards ensuring your child's success.

PARENT TO PARENT

"Both of our children worked hard at their studies and at their jobs during those years. Two different people, two different routes to the land of college degrees. Both with the same happy results. Sometimes the road was smooth, sometimes rough and full of potholes and detours. But the point is this: they knew where they were going and didn't give up until they got there. It was worth the trip."

"Any suggestions for parents just starting on the education highway? Yes, don't get discouraged, don't let up on the messages of encouragement (even when you're full of doubt), and keep the care packages going out."

"Is it worth it? Yes. Will they appreciate all that you have done for them? I believe they will, but even if they don't, that's not what you are doing it for anyway."

CAREER
EXPLORATION

25
"HOT"
CAREERS

The following pages contain 25 careers that can be considered "hot" careers. According to the Occupational Outlook Handbook, these careers have the the fastest growth, lowest unemployment, and the highest pay. These projections are for 1996 through 2006. most of these are summarized directly from the OOH.

When examining careers that are not included on this list, be sure to include the kind of information that is listed in these career sheets.

CAREER:
Systems analyst

DESCRIPTION:
A systems analyst is a computer professional who is responsible for designing, building, and servicing a system of hardware and software that will meet the needs of a particular organization.

TRAINING:
Most companies who hire systems analysts will require applicants to have a bachelor's degree in computer science, information science, or computer information systems. Those with a management information science (MIS) degree will be preferred by some companies and will also increase their earning potential.

EXPERIENCE:
Most companies will prefer applicants who have experience in the type of industry that they are involved. For example, if applying to a hospital, it would be valuable for the applicant to have volunteered, in some fashion, or completed an internship at a local hospital.

EMPLOYABILITY TRAITS:
strong problem solving skills
analytical skills
good interpersonal skills
communication skills
time management skills
attention to detail
independence
team worker
willingness to learn

SALARY INFORMATION:
The average salary job applicants with a bachelor's degree in systems analysis in 1997 was $43,800.

JOB OUTLOOK:
One of the three fastest growing occupations through the year 2006.

CAREER:
General managers and top executives

DESCRIPTION:
These individuals create general policies and also direct the operations of businesses, corporations, non-profit corporations, and government agencies.

TRAINING:
Many have bachelor's degrees in liberal arts or business administration. Obtaining a master's degree in business or specific related master's degree will make applicants more competitive. These would include the following: master's in engineering, master's in health services administration, master's in education administration, master's in public administration, and others.

EXPERIENCE:
Many general managers have experience at lower levels within the company and work their way up. Others transfer from similar companies.

EMPLOYABILITY TRAITS:
leadership
self-confidence
self-motivated
decision making skills
flexibility
communication skills
sound business judgment
stamina

SALARY INFORMATION:
Salaries vary greatly. General managers and top executives are among the highest paid workers in the country.

JOB OUTLOOK:
Average growth is expected, but because there are already so many positions, availability should be strong.

CAREER:
Registered nurses

DESCRIPTION:
Registered nurses are health care professionals who provide direct patient care, educate patients and families, assist physicians, administer medications, and develop and manage nursing care plans.

TRAINING:
Registered nurses must graduate from a nursing program and pass a national licensing examination. Associate degrees (ADN) are offered by community colleges and junior colleges. Diploma programs, usually 2-3 years, are offered by hospitals. Bachelor's degrees (BSN) are offered by colleges and universities. The BSN is the wave of the future.

EXPERIENCE:
Provided by nursing program. Volunteering in the health-care profession would help.

EMPLOYABILITY TRAITS:
emotional stability
caring and sympathetic
ability to accept responsibility
leadership
ability to follow orders
problem-solving skills

SALARY INFORMATION:
In 1996 the average salary for full time registered nurses was just over $36,000.

JOB OUTLOOK:
Employment of registered nurses is expected to grow faster than the average through the year 2006, and because the occupation is large, many new jobs will result.

CAREER:
Teachers, secondary education

DESCRIPTION:
Teachers act as facilitators or coaches, using interactive discussions and "hands-on" learning to help students learn and apply concepts in subjects such as science, mathematics, English, etc..

TRAINING:
All states require a bachelor's degree and completion of an approved teacher training program with a prescribed number of subject and education credits and supervised practice teaching. Some states may require a master's degree.

EXPERIENCE:
Provided by teaching program.

EMPLOYABILITY TRAITS:
creativity
familiarity with computers
patience
willingness to learn
strong communication skills
integrity
organization skills
problem-solving skills
ability to work in teams
ability to motivate
willing to relocate

SALARY INFORMATION:
During the 1995-1996 school year, secondary school teachers averaged about $38,000 a year.

JOB OUTLOOK:
Varies greatly depending on geography. Overall, employment of teachers is expected to increase as fast as average.

CAREER:
Clerical supervisors and managers

DESCRIPTION:
Clerical supervisors and managers coordinate the effective clerical administrative support for an organization.

TRAINING:
Many employers require post-secondary training -- in some cases an associate's or bachelor's degree.

EXPERIENCE:
Experience as an administrative assistant, secretary, or clerk will be helpful. Many clerical supervisors and managers are promoted from within.

EMPLOYABILITY TRAITS:
team work skills
determination
loyalty
poise
confidence
the ability to organize and prioritize
motivational skills
flexibility
a broad base of office skills, including computers

SALARY INFORMATION:
Median annual earnings of full-time clerical supervisors were about $28,900 in 1996. Employers in major metropolitan areas tend to pay higher salaries than those in rural areas.

JOB OUTLOOK:
Employment of clerical supervisors and managers is expected to grow about as fast as the average for all occupations through the year 2006. Most openings will occur due to replacement needs.

CAREER:
Database administrators and computer support specialists

DESCRIPTION:
Database administrators work with database management systems software, coordinating changes to, testing, and implementing computer databases. They also plan and coordinate security measures. Computer support specialists provide assistance and advice to users. They interpret problems and provide technical support for hardware, software, and systems.

TRAINING:
While there is no universally acceptable way to prepare for a job as a computer professional because employers' preferences depend on the work to be done, a bachelor's degree is virtually a prerequisite for most positions. Database administrators need a degree in computer science, information science, computer information systems, or data processing. Computer support specialists also need a degree in a computer-related field as well as experience and programming skills.

EXPERIENCE:
Experience with a variety of computer programming languages and systems is desirable.

EMPLOYABILITY TRAITS:
analytical
problem-solving skills
good communication skills
logical thinker
ability to concentrate
attention to detail
ability to work independently
ability to work with a team
willingness to learn

SALARY INFORMATION:
Mid to high $30's.

JOB OUTLOOK:
Expected to be among the three fastest growing occupations through the year 2006.

41

CAREER:
Maintenance repairers

DESCRIPTION:
Maintenance repairers are responsible for the maintenance and repair of machinery found in plants, factories, or businesses. They diagnose, disassemble, repair, replace, and test machinery. They may also be responsible for the installation of new machinery.

TRAINING:
Many workers learn their trade through a 4-year apprenticeship program. These programs are usually sponsored by a local trade union.

EXPERIENCE:
high school courses in mechanical drawing, mathematics, blueprint reading, physics, and electronics are especially useful.

EMPLOYABILITY TRAITS:
good physical conditioning
agility
mechanical aptitude
manual dexterity
problem-solving skills

SALARY INFORMATION:
Median monthly earnings for full-time industrial machinery repairers was about $29,000.

JOB OUTLOOK:
Employment of industrial machinery repairers is projected to grow more slowly than average for all occupations through the year 2006. Nevertheless, applicants with broad skills in machine repair should have favorable job prospects.

CAREER:
Teacher, special education

DESCRIPTION:
Special education teachers work with children and youth who have a variety of disabilities. These disabilities include specific learning disabilities, mental retardation, speech or language impairment, serious emotional disturbance, visual and hearing impairment, orthopedic impairment, autism, traumatic brain injury, and multiple disabilities.

TRAINING:
All states require a bachelor's degree and completion of an approved teacher preparation program with a prescribed number of subject and education credits and supervised practice testing. Specialization and licensing are also required.

EXPERIENCE:
Provided by teaching program. (Volunteering with special needs students is recommended -- this career can be very emotionally demanding.)

EMPLOYABILITY TRAITS:
patience
motivational skills
ability to accept differences
communication skills
ability to work in teams

SALARY INFORMATION:
The average salary in 1995-96 was $37,900.

JOB OUTLOOK:
Special education teachers have excellent job prospects, as many school districts report shortages of qualified teachers. Positions in rural areas and cities are more plentiful than suburban or wealthy urban areas. Job opportunities may be better in certain specialties such as language impairments and learning disabilities. Overall growth will be faster than average through the year 2006.

CAREER:
Computer engineers

DESCRIPTION:
Computer engineers work with hardware and software aspects of systems design and development. They emphasize the development of prototypes and often work as part of a team that designs new computing devices or computer-related equipment, systems, or software. Hardware engineers work with computer hardware -- for example, chips or device controllers. Software engineers design software and software packages.

TRAINING:
Computer hardware engineers generally require a bachelor's degree in computer engineering or electrical engineering. Software engineers need a degree in computer science.

EXPERIENCE:
Experience with a variety of programming languages, systems, and technologies is desired. Internships and co-op programs are recommended.

EMPLOYABILITY TRAITS:
logical thinker
problem-solving skills
good communication skills
ability to organize and prioritize
ability to concentrate
attention to detail
ability to work independently and in teams

SALARY INFORMATION:
Graduates with a bachelor's degree in computer engineering averaged about $39,722 per year in 1997.

JOB OUTLOOK:
One of the three fastest growing occupations through the year 2006.

CAREER:
Social workers

DESCRIPTION:
Social workers are people who help other people deal with their relationships, solve their personal, family, and community problems, and learn to cope with social and environmental forces affecting their daily lives. There is a variety of social workers. Social workers can deal with child welfare or family services and adult protective services. Other occupational fields in social work include mental health, health care, school, criminal justice, occupational, and gerontological.

TRAINING:
A bachelor's degree in social work is preferred. Undergraduate majors in psychology, sociology, and related fields satisfy some hiring requirements. A master's degree in social work (MSW) is necessary for positions in health, mental health, supervisory, administrative and staff training positions. All states and the District of Columbia have licensing certification or registration laws regarding social work practice and the use of professional titles.

EXPERIENCE:
Volunteering or internships in social service environments are recommended.

EMPLOYABILITY TRAITS:
emotional maturity
objectivity
sensitivity
responsibility
ability to work independently
problem-solving skills

SALARY INFORMATION:
In 1997, social workers with a BSW earned about $25,000, while social workers with an MSW had median earnings of about $35,000.

JOB OUTLOOK:
Faster than average through the year 2006.

CAREER:
Food service managers

DESCRIPTION:
Food service managers are responsible for the efficient and profitable operation of restaurant or institutional food service facilities. They select and price menu items, achieve consistent quality in food preparation and service, and recruit, train, and supervise employees.

TRAINING:
Although some positions are filled by promotion from within, those applicants possessing a bachelor's or associate's degree in hospitality management will have an advantage.

EXPERIENCE:
Experience in a restaurant or food service and preparation environment is an advantage. Most training programs will include internships to provide this experience.

EMPLOYABILITY TRAITS:
good health and stamina
self-discipline
initiative
leadership
problem-solving skills
attention to detail
good communication skills
neat and clean appearance

SALARY INFORMATION:
Average annual salaries were about $23,900 in 1996.

JOB OUTLOOK:
Job opportunities will be best for those with associate's or bachelor's degrees and growth should be faster than average.

CAREER:
Hotel managers

DESCRIPTION:
Hotel managers are responsible for the efficient and profitable operation of their establishments. They set room rates, allocate funds to various departments, approve expenditures, establish standards for service to guests, and organize meeting and banquet facilities.

TRAINING:
Post-secondary training in hotel or restaurant management is preferred. Associate's and bachelor's degrees are available. Those possessing liberal arts degrees with significant hotel-related experience can also find employment.

EXPERIENCE:
Experience working in a hotel environment is a plus. Many training programs will provide opportunities for experience.

EMPLOYABILITY TRAITS:
familiarity with computers
great people skills
problem-solving skills
attention to detail
initiative
self-discipline
organizational skills
leadership skills
strong communication skills

SALARY INFORMATION:
There is a great deal of variety, but the average salary in 1996 was around $40,000.

JOB OUTLOOK:
Growth will be as fast as average through the year 2006. There will also be a large number of openings due to replacement needs.

CAREER:
College and university faculty

DESCRIPTION:
College and university professors prepare lectures, exercises, laboratory experiments, grade exams and papers, and advise and work with students individually. Faculty at larger universities may also conduct research and give lectures to professional organizations.

TRAINING:
A Ph.D. is generally required for full-time positions in four-year colleges and universities. In two-year institutions, master's degree holders may qualify.

EXPERIENCE:

EMPLOYABILITY TRAITS:
inquiring and analytical minds
strong desire to pursue and disseminate knowledge
strong communication skills
integrity
independence

SALARY INFORMATION:
Salaries for college and university professors averaged $51,000.

JOB OUTLOOK:
Employment for college and university professors is expected to increase about as fast as average.

CAREER:
Engineering, science, and computer systems Managers

DESCRIPTION:
Engineering, science, and computer systems managers are responsible for planning, coordinating, and directing research, development, design, production and computer-related activities.

TRAINING:
Most managers have a bachelor's, master's, or Ph.D. in their specific field. Possessing a degree in business administration or management in addition to a technical degree can also be an asset.

EXPERIENCE:
Experience as an engineer, mathematician, scientist, or computer professional is usually required to become a engineering, science, or computer systems manager.

EMPLOYABILITY TRAITS:
above average technical skills
leadership skills
communication skills
decision-making skills
time management skills
organizational skills
people skills
motivational skills

SALARY INFORMATION:
Engineering, Science, or Computer System Managers salaries can range from $33,000 to well over $100,000. Managers often earn 15% to 20% more than those that they supervise.

JOB OUTLOOK:
Employment for these managers is expected to increase much faster than the average through the year 2006.

49

CAREER:
Licensed practical nurses

DESCRIPTION:
Licensed practical nurses or licensed vocational nurses are responsible for providing basic bedside care. Under the direction of physicians and registered nurses they may take vital signs, provide much of the "hands on" care, observe patients, and help them with daily physical and emotional needs.

TRAINING:
Most practical nursing programs last about one year and are administered by technical or vocational schools, community and junior colleges, some high schools, hospitals, and colleges and universities. All states will require L.P.N.s to pass a licensing examination after completing the program.

EXPERIENCE:
Provided by state approved programs.

EMPLOYABILITY TRAITS:
caring and sympathetic attitude
emotional stability
ability to work in a team
ability to follow orders

SALARY INFORMATION:
Median annual earnings of full-time salaried licensed practical nurses in 1996 were $24,336.

JOB OUTLOOK:
Employment of licensed practical nurses should improve faster than the average through the year 2006. Most openings will occur in nursing homes.

CAREER:
Financial managers

DESCRIPTION:
Financial managers prepare financial reports, oversee the flow of cash and financial instruments, monitor the extension of credit, asses the risk of transactions, raise capital, analyze investments, develop financial status information, and communicate this information. They can be chief financial officers, vice-presidents of finance, treasurers, controllers, credit managers, or cash managers.

TRAINING:
A bachelor's or master's degree in finance, accounting, economics or business administration is required. A master's degree is preferred.

EXPERIENCE:
Most financial managers will be promoted from a pool of people having experience in the field. Gaining experience during or after college in a financial function is a must.

EMPLOYABILITY TRAITS:
willingness to learn
leadership skills
ability to work independently
people skills
attention to detail
strong communication skills

SALARY INFORMATION:
The median annual salary for financial managers was $40,700 in 1996. Those with a master's degree in business administration averaged $10,900 more than those with a bachelor's degree.

JOB OUTLOOK:
Employment is expected to increase as fast as average through the year 2006.

CAREER:
Marketing, advertising and public relations managers

DESCRIPTION:
Marketing, advertising, and public relations managers usually supervise a staff that is responsible for sales, communication, promotion, and marketing research.

TRAINING:
A bachelor's or master's degree in sociology, psychology, literature, philosophy, liberal arts, business administration, marketing, advertising, or journalism can prepare individuals for these positions. Course work should include classes in marketing, consumer behavior, market research, sales, communications, and visual arts.

EXPERIENCE:
Most marketing, advertising and public relations managers are promoted from within. This experience can be gained during or after college.

EMPLOYABILITY TRAITS:
emotional maturity
creativity
ability to work independently
ability to handle stress
flexibility
decisiveness
very strong communication skills
ability to persuade

SALARY INFORMATION:
The median annual salary of marketing, advertising, and public relations managers was $46,000 in 1996.

JOB OUTLOOK:
Employment is expected to increase faster than average through the year 2006.

CAREER:
Computer programmers

DESCRIPTION:
Computer programmers write, test, and maintain detailed instructions (software or programs) that list in a logical order the steps computers must execute to perform their functions.

TRAINING:
Most programmers (45.2%) will have a bachelor's degree in computer science, mathematics or information systems. Some will have college training in programming but no degree (20.9%), a graduate degree (14.2%), a high school degree or less (10%), or an associate's degree (9.6%).

EXPERIENCE:
In the absence of a degree, substantial specialized experience or expertise may be needed. Even with a degree, experience is highly advantageous.

EMPLOYABILITY TRAITS:
the ability to work independently
the ability to work in a team
willingness to learn
flexibility
creativity
problem-solving skills

SALARY INFORMATION:
Median earnings of programmers who worked full-time during 1996 were about $40,500 per year.

JOB OUTLOOK:
Employment of programmers should increase faster than average through the year 2006.

CAREER:
Instructors and coaches
sports and physical training

DESCRIPTION:
These instructors and coaches are responsible for teaching groups the right ways of performing exercise and other fitness-related activities. They will teach, supervise, and correct their students.

TRAINING:
1 to 12 months of on-the-job training

EXPERIENCE:

EMPLOYABILITY TRAITS:

SALARY INFORMATION:

JOB OUTLOOK:
Much faster than average

CAREER:
Lawyers

DESCRIPTION:
Lawyers interpret the law and then apply it to specific situations. They may act as advocates, representing a client in litigation, or as advisors giving legal counsel. Much of a lawyer's time will be spent researching and then communicating pertinent information. Most lawyers are still in private practice and handle civil or criminal cases.

TRAINING:
Potential lawyers must first obtain a bachelor's degree. Courses in English, foreign language, public speaking, government, philosophy, history, economics, mathematics, and computer science are useful. They must then be accepted by and graduate from an accredited law school. The final step will be passing a written bar examination.

EXPERIENCE:
Part-time or summer clerkships, as well as programs offered by the law schools will be helpful.

EMPLOYABILITY TRAITS:
responsibility
people skills
perseverance
reasoning ability
creativity
strong communication skills

SALARY INFORMATION:
The median annual salary of all lawyers was about $60,000.

JOB OUTLOOK:
About as fast as average.

CAREER:
Physicians

DESCRIPTION:
Physicians diagnose illnesses as well as prescribe and administer treatments for those illnesses. Physicians also educate and counsel their patients about health-related issues. Physicians are either M.D.s (Doctors of medicine) or D.O.s (Doctors of Osteopathic Medicine). While the differences between these two types of physicians are dwindling, the D.O. traditionally focuses on the musculo-skeletal system, preventative medicine, and holistic health. There are many specialties of medicine in which physicians may select to specialize.

TRAINING:
Most applicants to medical school will have a bachelor's degree in biology, chemistry, or other health-related major. Med schools will accept students with other majors provided the necessary course work has been completed. Med school applicants will also have to complete the MEDCAT test. Physicians will complete four years of medical school followed by a 2-6 year residency.

EXPERIENCE:
Volunteering in a hospital or other health care facility can help students get accepted to medical school.

EMPLOYABILITY TRAITS:
desire to serve patients
ability to work independently
perseverance
strong communication skills
emotional stability
decision-making/problem-solving skills
willingness to learn
flexibility

SALARY INFORMATION:
Residents can make from $32, 789 to $40, 849. According to the American Medical Association, M.D.s averaged $160,000 for 1995.
JOB OUTLOOK:
Faster than average growth.

CAREER:
Electrical and electronics engineers

DESCRIPTION:
Electrical and electronics engineers, develop, design, test, and supervise the manufacture of electrical and electronic equipment. Electrical equipment includes power generating and transmission equipment used by electric utilities, the electric motors, machinery controls, and lighting and wiring in buildings, automobiles, and aircraft. Electronic equipment includes radar, computer hardware, and communications and video equipment.

TRAINING:
Most electrical and electronics engineers will have a bachelor's degree in electrical engineering.

EXPERIENCE:
Having a part-time job in an industry dealing with electronics or electrical engineering can be helpful.

EMPLOYABILITY TRAITS:
creativity
willingness to learn
analytical
attention to detail
ability to work in a team
good communication skills

SALARY INFORMATION:
The median annual earnings for electrical engineers were $51,700.

JOB OUTLOOK:
Employment for electrical and electronics engineers is expected to increase faster than average through the year 2006.

CAREER:
Career corrections officers

DESCRIPTION:
Career corrections officers are responsible for overseeing individuals who have been arrested, are awaiting trial or other hearing, or who have been convicted of a crime and sentenced to serve time in a jail, reformatory, or penitentiary. They maintain security and observe inmate conduct and behavior to prevent disturbances and escapes.

TRAINING:
Most institutions require that corrections officers be at least 18 or 21 years of age, have a high school education or its equivalent, have no felony convictions, and be a United States citizen. Increasingly, institutions are requiring some post secondary education in psychology, criminal justice, criminology, and related fields.

EXPERIENCE:
Provided by employer.

EMPLOYABILITY TRAITS:
good health and strength
good judgment
decision-making skills
patience
good communication skills

SALARY INFORMATION:
The average annual salaries for Federal and State corrections officers were $26,100 in 1996.

JOB OUTLOOK:
Employment of corrections officers is expected to increase faster than the average for all occupations through the year 2006. Layoffs of corrections officers are rare.

CAREER:
Securities and financial services sales representatives

DESCRIPTION:
The most important part of a sales representatives job is finding and building a customer base. Securities and financial services sales representatives sell stocks, bonds, shares in mutual funds, insurance annuities, or other financial products.

TRAINING:
Most of these sales representatives are college graduates with courses in business administration, economics, and finance. Sales representatives may also be required to seek special licenses before selling.

EXPERIENCE:
Usually provided by the employer.

EMPLOYABILITY TRAITS:
good sales ability
communication skills
professional appearance
highly motivated
self confidence
ability to work independently
willingness to learn

SALARY INFORMATION:
The median annual earnings of securities and financial services sales representatives in 1996 were about $38,800. Trainees are usually paid an hourly wage until they meet licensing and registration requirements. Securities sales representatives usually can make considerably more than financial sales representatives.

JOB OUTLOOK:
Although demand for securities sales representatives fluctuates as the economy expands and contracts, employment of securities sales representatives should grow much faster than average through the year 2006.

CAREER:
Physical therapists

DESCRIPTION:
Physical therapists provide services that help restore function, improve mobility, relieve pain, and prevent or limit permanent physical disabilities of patients suffering from injuries or disease. They restore, maintain, and promote overall fitness and health.

TRAINING:
By the year 2001 all accredited physical therapy programs will be at the master's degree level and above. Competition for entrance into physical therapist educational programs is very intense, so interested students should attain superior grades in high school and college especially in science courses, including anatomy, biology, chemistry, social sciences, mathematics, and physics.

EXPERIENCE:
Before granting admission, many professional education programs require experience as a volunteer in a physical therapy department of a hospital or clinic.

EMPLOYABILITY TRAITS:
strong interpersonal skills
compassion
willingness to learn
perseverance

SALARY INFORMATION:
According to the American Physical Therapist's Association's survey of physical therapists practicing in hospital settings, the medial annual base salary of full-time physical therapists was $48,000 in 1996.

JOB OUTLOOK:
Physical therapists are expected to be among the fastest growing occupations through the year 2006.

CAREER:
Artists and commercial artists

DESCRIPTION:
Artists and commercial artists communicate ideas, thoughts, and feelings through various methods and materials - including computers, oils, water colors, acrylics, pastels, magic markers, pencils, pen and ink, silk screen, plaster or clay, photographs, and sound.

TRAINING:
Artists and commercial artists can receive training at both 4-year and 2-year institutions. Increasing trends suggest that artists become proficient with computer art functions.

EXPERIENCE:
Internships or part-time jobs allow artists to develop a portfolio. A portfolio is a collection of samples of the artists work and often serves as a resume for artists.

EMPLOYABILITY TRAITS:
creativity
problem solving skills
familiarity with computers

SALARY INFORMATION:
Median earnings for salaried visual artists who usually worked full-time were about $27,100 per year in 1996. The Society of Publication Designers estimates that entry level graphic designers earned between $23,000 and $27,000 annually in 1997.

JOB OUTLOOK:
Visual artists held about 276,000 jobs in 1996. Nearly 6 out of 10 are self-employed.

FINDING OUT WHAT THE EMPLOYERS WANT

OK, let's move on to the next step ..... determining what employers want.

For each career that interests your child there is a standard set of qualifications and skills that employers will require. Finding out what those requirements are will be our next step. The reason we want to do this now boils down to a basic principle of salesmanship. If you want to sell something to somebody you must first know what that somebody needs. Likewise, since your child wants to sell him/herself to an employer he/she must first know what that employer needs.

AVOID COMMON MISTAKES

It is very important that we operate with an open mind as we begin to examine how to get your child to his/her career goal. You will find as we go through this process that there are ways to reach certain careers that you may not have thought of in the past. What I mean is that most parents are probably assuming at this point that when we are talking about what "employers want", we are talking about just a four-year degree. This will be the case for some careers, but not necessarily all careers. In fact, according to the U.S. Department of Labor, only 20 percent of all jobs will require a college degree by the year 2000. So, we must be willing to take a look at all options and not just colleges. I feel the need to emphasize this point because many parents and others involved with your child's future look at a degree, any degree, from a four year college as the key to success. It has become painfully clear that this is not always the case.

Another problem is that for years people have looked at a four-year degree from a college as a status symbol. Sure, any parent would be proud to say that his/her son or daughter is going to the most competitive and prestigious college in the state, or even one of the service academies, but what good will that be if after graduation your child is still not adequately prepared to do something for a living that they enjoy, and that will allow them to be financially independent?

Again, we must remember that our goal is to determine what skills and qualifications are necessary for employment in the careers that we have selected in the first section of this book. This will need to be done with each one of the possible careers that your child has listed.

Be sure to record on every sheet of paper in your career file what the qualifications and training are recommended. If you used several sources for information about each career make sure that each source and each training option is documented as you go.

WHAT DID YOUR SOURCES RECOMMEND?

We will start by returning to the same sources we used in selecting a career.

1) If you selected something from the newspaper, did that newspaper ad spell out what training was required? Read the ad again to see if it spelled-out a specific course of study or degree from a college or technical school. For example:
"Requires a <u>four-year degree</u> in <u>marketing</u>..."
"Prefer <u>associate's degree</u> in <u>electronics</u>..."

They might also spell out that they require a specific license or certification.

"Over the road drivers must have <u>CDL class A</u> license..."
"<u>Personal training certification</u> required..."

If you did use the paper for your source, and specific training or educational information was spelled out for you, you are well on your way to moving on to the next step. As you can see, when you know where to look, things can be far more easy than you ever imagined.

2) If you used or selected a career from the <u>Occupational Outlook Handbook,</u> turn to the section labeled "Training, Other Qualifications, and Advancement." (this book makes everything so easy). Read this section, and then record the training options recommended as well as any other qualifications suggested. Many of the careers that are described in this handbook will have several training options. List each one on your sheet and leave space around them so that you can take notes later.

3) If you were able to speak to someone in the career chosen by your child ...How did they get there? Did they get a degree from a college or technical school? Did they use a combination of training options? This is a great way of examining training options, because here is a person who has already "been there and done that". After finding out how they got to this point in their careers, ask them if they would do it the same way if given the chance to do it again. Also ask them if there are other ways to to get into that career field, and what are the advantages and disadvantages of the different training options. Remember to take what you hear with a bit of skepticism. The information that you get from an actual person will be slightly more biased than what you would get from a source like the Occupational Outlook Handbook. Again, make sure that you record the options given to you on you career sheet.

4) If you spoke to a teacher of a related subject, does that teacher know what is required in order to do that specific career. While you are dealing with school officials check with the guidance counselors. They've seen hundreds if not thousands of young people take off towards different careers. They will be able to add some light on the different vehicles used by students in the past.

LOOK FOR THE SPECIFICS

While you are inquiring about the qualifications and training required by your child's career choices, make sure that you look for the specifics. As I have mentioned earlier the most employable people are the ones who have the exact qualifications for which the employers are looking. The job market has become increasingly specialized, and those people who realize this and adjust will be the most employable. The following is a list of things you want to take note of. As you come across each of these specifics make sure that you record them on the appropriate career sheet.

1) What degree is required? (A professional degree, a master's degree, a bachelor's degree, an associate's degree)

2) If a degree is required, what subject must that degree be in? (Accounting, Electronics, Engineering, Medical Technology, etc.)

3) What certifications or licenses are required? (CPA, CDL class A license, CNA certification, etc.)

4) What equipment or computer software must your child be familiar with? (Lotus notes, UNIX, WAN, AUTOCAD, etc.)

5) What personal qualities must your child possess? (Communication skills, willing to work outside job description, willing to work long hours, strong math skills, good people skills, etc.)

6) What working experience and how much of that experience is required?

GETTING WHAT EMPLOYERS WANT

GENERAL TRAITS OF EMPLOYABILITY

While most careers will have very definite qualifications that are specific to to that particular career. Many careers will also share qualifications. These we will call "General Traits of Employability". These are the traits that are desired by just about every employer no matter what positions that employer is trying to fill. As we go through these characteristics, see which ones your child already possesses and which ones your child needs to develop. You will find a checklist at the end of this section that may be helpful. Your child should use this form to perform a self-evaluation of his/her general traits of employability. Feel free to photocopy this checklist so that your son or daughter can have teachers, and, if they have had a part-time job, former employers complete the form.

1. Skills

The primary factor that will determine if your child will be employable is what skills he/she possesses. By a skill I mean what it is that they "can do" for an employer. The more that your child "can do" - the more he/she will be employable. To be employable in a particular career your child will need to find out just what employers in that particular field want their employees to be able to do, and then make sure that he/she learns how to do those things. Using the same sources that you used to select a career, find out what theses "can do's" are. In many cases they will involve equipment or computer software.

Many students in the past have made the mistake of trying to enter the job market with just a whole lot of information about a whole lot of things. Sure, being informed is good, but it does not necessarily make you employable. As you prepare to make your child employable, pay particular attention to these "can do's". Record them on your career sheet, and make sure that, as your child finishes high school and selects training options, he/she will be getting these skills.

One of the primary reasons why employers will ask for certain licenses is that these licenses imply that the person carrying them "can do" certain things. Many associate and bachelor's degrees carry this same implication.

Some of the other characteristics that we will discuss in this section will actually be skills, but in many cases are not thought of as such.

2. The ability to communicate effectively

One of the most desirable characteristics in an employee is the ability to communicate effectively. If you doubt this, pick up a Sunday paper and scan through the help-wanted ads. Across the board, no matter what the career field, you will see employers using precious space in their ads asking for effective communicators. When employers talk about communication skills they are talking about four different things.

The ability to read well. By this I mean the ability to read for content and understanding. Employers want employees who can read manuals, memos, and other instructions, and be able understand and act on what was written. The best way to help your child to develop this would be to encourage them to read...as much and as often as possible. Subscribe to magazines that address your child's interests. Visit local bookstores with your child to encourage them to purchase books that he/she will actually read.

The ability to write well. Because so much communication in business and industry is done through the written word, and also because words on paper are sometimes the first and only exposure one business might have with another business, it is very important that what your child writes is correct and clearly communicates the intended message. Encouraging your child to write letters, e-mail, or even keep a diary are great ways to keep this skill sharp.

The ability to speak well. By speaking well I mean two things. First, the ability to speak to another person, especially a stranger, one-on-one, and clearly state a message without mumbling, stammering, or straying. And second, the ability to stand before a group and deliver an effective message. Encourage your child to join clubs or organizations that require this. One of the requirements at Fishburne Military School, my high school alma-matter, was that every cadet speak in front of the whole corps several times per year. At the time I hated it. Now, I can honestly say that this was one of the most valuable educational experiences of my life.

71

The ability to listen well. Effective listeners are valuable because they don't have to be told something twice. Effective listening requires the discipline to focus your thoughts on what is being said as well as what is meant. Effective note-taking skills require that you not just write what was is said, but extract the important information from what is said. This is great practice for effective listening. If your child does not take notes in his/her classes, or does not know how to take notes, enroll him/her in a study-skills class. In these classes, students will be coached on how to pull-out and record meaning from what is being said - great listening skills practice.

All through high school your child will have the opportunity to practice these communication skills. Special consideration has to be placed on his/her performance in English classes. English teachers will provide your child with the instruction and practice he/she will need, but how much good that instruction does depends on how seriously your child takes this instruction. Encourage your children to pay particular attention to this subject in high school. Poor communication skills can severely limit their ability to succeed. This again can be a benefit of having selected a specific career goal. If you show them that their dream job requires that they be effective communicators, they will begin to see the value of English classes. Again, in many cases you cannot just tell teenagers to do well in a particular class, you must show them why they need to do well in a particular class.

3. The ability to work with numbers

Not all careers will require that your son or daughter be a Calculus wizard, but a great many will require your child to have strong math skills. Careers dealing with technology, dealing with money, and dealing with statistics of any kind will require strong math skills. So, the safest bet when dealing with how much math is necessary would be "as much as possible, with a strong emphasis on the basics".

The best practice for using math in the work force would be "the dreaded word problem". Most kids hate word problems, but they are great practice for the actual applications of math in the real world.

As a parent you have the opportunity to help during the high school years and even before that. Your child will have homework from their math classes. If you can, encourage your child to go further than the actual assignment, especially in the section of the assignment dealing with word problems. Your child's math teacher will love you. Enthusiastic students are a blessing to those in education.

4. Familiarity with computers

More and more of the work force is becoming computerized. Even if your son or daughter will not be working directly in the computer field, he/she can expect to work with a computer in some aspect of the job. If you look at the want-ads you will see the number of jobs that will require your child to have experience with various software programs or pieces of hardware. The more experience your son or daughter can get on the computer, and the earlier he or she can get this experience, the better.

If you don't yet have a computer at home, it would be a great idea to get one. If money is a concern, consider buying a less sophisticated computer, or even one that has been used. You might as well get one for your child now, especially if they will be considering higher education. No student should enter college or technical school these days without a computer. Libraries also have computers that are available for public use.

Every student should take at least one computer course in high school. If you can't enroll your child in a computer course at your local school consider an evening course at a community college.

If you are looking at higher education, one thing that you might consider is the possibility of having your child select a computer specialty as a minor. Not only would this help your child to market themselves in the field of their major, but could also serve as a back-up if he/she can't find their primary career choice immediately after graduation.

5. The ability and willingness to work in a team

A big trend in business and industry is the movement towards teams. Recent times have seen the end of the person who works in a little hole and comes in contact with his co-workers only at the coffee machine. Instead, your child can expect to work with a group of people whose functions are tightly intertwined and come together to achieve the goals of that group.

Strong interpersonal skills, the ability to get along with all kinds of people, and experience working in teams combine to make your child very attractive to the increasing number of employers who have adopted the team approach.

Don't let your child be a loner. Encourage him/her to join an athletic team, a club, get a job working with other people, or at the very least get out of the house and interact with friends. I have seen so many kids these days that are turning into "termites". They hide in their rooms, watching TV or playing video games, and almost never leave the house. When you look at them they appear as if they would shrivel-up and die if ever hit by a ray of sunshine. We know that this is bad for kids overall development, but is also bad for their employability.

Encouraging this participation as early in your child's development as possible is the best. As kids get older, they have a more difficult time working in groups and joining teams if they haven't had the chance to do so earlier.

6. Attendance, attendance, attendance

When an employer hires your child, they want to be able to count on him/her to be there. Your children will find little tolerance for absenteeism in the work force. Some employers even frown on the use of sick-days and have devised certain reward systems for people who don't use those sick-days. Other employers rely on more traditional methods...they fire you!

When speaking to employers, I have found many who where passionate about the subject. I even ran into an employer recently who actually checks high school attendance records when hiring engineers.

Poor attendance can sabotage the most talented and skilled job applicants. After all, what good is the highly intelligent, highly skilled, team player... if he/she doesn't show? Stress this to your child. A poor attendance record in school or at his/her part-time jobs can come back to haunt your child.

My parents were always big believers in this. I can still recall a common early-morning conversation between my parents and myself....

Me, "Mom...Dad...I don't feel good. I'm not going to school today."
Them, "Are you Dying?"
Me, "Not yet."
Them, "Are you bleeding?"
Me, "Not externally."
Them, "Can you feel your legs?"
Me, "Wait a minute...........yes."
Them, "Then get your butt out of bed!"

Thanks. Really!

7. A willingness to learn

Change and progress are the realities of today's business world. In order for companies to succeed they must be able to keep up with this change. If a company does not keep up with new technology they will never be able to compete with their state-of-the-art competitors. To do this, companies must employ people with a willingness to learn - people who have the ability and desire to keep up with all the changes in technology. In fact, more and more companies today offer tuition assistance to those employees who are willing to continue their education.

The saying "Learning is a lifetime process", has never been more true. Demonstrating this trait to an employer by encouraging your child to take his/her education seriously, and encouraging your child to continue his/her education in any way, can help to open many doors for your child.

When speaking about this subject with job-hunters, I will always encourage them to ask questions during the interview. These questions should demonstrate a genuine curiosity about the company and its future or even your child's future at that company. During the interviews that I have personally conducted, I have always been more impressed with those applicants who have well though-out, serious questions. While asking questions can be a good thing, always avoid asking questions about vacations or time off. Remember, too, that showing a willingness to learn by asking questions during the interview is a trick that can be used, but can't replace the impression made by furthering one's education.

8. A positive attitude

People with negative attitudes are "brakes". They slow an organization down and interfere with it's smooth operation. Some of what employers do in the hiring process is try and weed out those people with negative attitudes.

A common method would be asking a prospective employee about an old job or old employers. The most common mistake made in this situation is to complain. In many cases employers may actually be trying to see how easily they can draw complaint out of an employee. If they can draw-out that complaint easily, they can safely assume that this person is comfortable with complaint. If this person is comfortable with complaint, he/she is probably the kind of person who complains a lot. If this person complains a lot, then this person is probably somebody who tends to look at the negative in a situation before looking at the positive.

Another test that is used involves putting a prospective employee in an impossible hypothetical dilemma and asking that prospective employee how he/she might get out of that situation, or how they might solve the problem. In many cases there won't be a solution to the problem. What the employer will be looking for is "the try". In other words, is this person willing to give it a try, or will he/she just throw up his/her arms and quit. Obviously employers are looking for the person who sees the possibility that it <u>can</u> be done, instead of the person who sees the possibility that it <u>can't</u> be done.

Helping your child to understand this, and encouraging him/her to develop a pattern of looking for the good in a situation before looking for the bad can really pay off in the job market.

Teenagers are the biggest complainers around. Pardon my language, but the phrase "this sucks" is the battle cry of many high school students. It's part of the questioning process. Having patience and helping children to see the reason (the "why") in a situation can help to alleviate that attitude... temporarily.

9. Independence

"Corporate downsizing" and "trimming the fat" have become commonplace in today's world of business and industry. One of the consequences of this is the reduction or even elimination of the middle-level manager. With less supervisors a new emphasis has been placed on hiring people who don't need as much supervision. This ability to work without supervision has always been a desired trait in new employees, but never more so than now.

When employers are looking at your child, they will be looking for the kind of person who can be given an assignment and a deadline, and then be trusted to get it done, without having to be reminded or cajoled. Trustworthiness, honesty, and initiative are a large part of being independent.

When you think about it, this is the best kind of job to have. Anyone who has ever worked for an overbearing boss knows how great it is to be trusted and left alone. In order to get this kind of opportunity your child will have to first earn it.

There are plenty of chances to practice and prove this during high school. Parents need to look for those opportunities, and gradually give their children opportunities to experience independence. Children who never have the opportunity to operate independently often grow up to be adults and employees who need a great deal of supervision, or who self-destruct when given the chance to be independent.

10. Flexibility

This is an extremely important trait for anyone entering the job market today. The reason is that a large number of opportunities for your child will be created by small businesses. Small business have to stay flexible in order to compete against the big businesses. In fact this flexibility is one of the advantages of being a small business. In order to stay flexible, small businesses need to hire people who are equally as flexible.

One thing that your child needs to be comfortable with is working outside this/her job description. Employers don't want the person who will tie the companies hands, instead they want the kind of person who is willing to do whatever it takes to get the job done. Understanding the importance and value of being open-minded and flexible in today's job market will greatly increase your child's chances of being hired and being successful.

11. The ability to organize and prioritize

Complex tasks and confusing situations are best handled step-by-step. This ability to effectively break down a difficult task into bits and pieces, organize those bits and pieces, and then decide which bit will be done first, and which piece will be done last is a rare and valuable skill. All high school students have this ability to some degree. They carry loads and juggle schedules and responsibilities that make most adult's heads spin. They come up short sometimes selecting what activities will take priority over others, but that improves with maturity.

The more practice they have doing this the better. Encourage them to participate and be involved, but be prepared to help them with the priorities.

12. Leadership

We are definitely in need of leaders in industry as well as society. Not the kind of leader who can lead because they have a title or some kind of position, but the kind of leader who can emerge from a group and say things like, "Why don't we do it this way?" or, "That's going to screw things up. Why don't we go around this situation?"

To demonstrate the need for leaders, picture this - It's Friday or Saturday night -- you are out with your husband, wife, sweetie... What is the typical response to this question? -- "So, what do you want to do?" In most cases the response will be, "I don't know. What do you want to do?" If no one is willing to take the leadership role in this situation, nothing gets done, and it's another night in front of "the tube".

So few people are willing to take the leadership role. They fear ridicule or don't want to take the responsibility for their actions if something goes wrong. Many people are content to keep a low profile and just go with the flow. Too many of these people in an organization, and that organization goes nowhere. And, so, the need for effective leaders.

Where will these leaders come from? Well, the people who have had the opportunity to lead in the past are the people who will lead in the future.

While your child is still developing, encourage him/her to seek out leadership opportunities, both formal and informal. When employers see this in your child, they'll see not just a future employee, but a future manager.

13. The ability to solve problems

Business is all about solving problems - your own or someone else's. Those who get hired to solve these problems, and those who are successful at solving those problems, are effective at doing four things.

1. Acknowledging that there is a problem.
   (Things could be better)

2. Identifying that problem.
   (Separating that problem from it's symptoms)

3. Coming up with a plan to solve that problem.

and

4. Acting on that plan.
   (Perhaps the most important step)

Using these four steps, your child can solve any problem. And, as you already know, teenagers will have their share of problems. Help your child practice solving his/her own problems using these four steps. Your child will become more employable with every problem he/she can overcome.

14. Confidence

Everyone is impressed by a confident, self-assured, young adult. When such a person approaches you squarely, looks you in the eye, shakes your hand, and clearly introduce him/herself, you cannot help but see success. This is what we associate with confidence -- success.

Most people would rather spend time with successful people than with unsuccessful people. Employers are the same way. There is a catch. In order to spend time with your confident, self-assured child... they have to hire him or her.

Confidence can be harder for your child to achieve than you might first think. High school students are brutal. Every day they endure a barrage of peer insults, and spend much of their time reminding each other of their failures and short-comings. Most adults would crack in this kind of environment, but somehow young people find a way to endure.

Enduring, however, does not translate into confidence. Anything you can do to recognize your child's genuine successes and strengths helps. Parents need to encourage children to take on challenges so that they have the chance to succeed. Parents also need to show their children that if they fail, they must again take on another challenge, another chance to succeed. We should do this not just for their employability, but also for their over all well being.

BEFORE YOU MOVE ON

Before you move on in the process of getting what employers want, you will need to have completed everything in this section. Make sure that you now know exactly what the employers will want when hiring for your child's career choice. Also, make sure that your child and some of the people who know your child have completed the employability checklist. By doing these two things your child will know what they have, and what they need. Knowing these things will make your training choices far more effective.

The employability trait check-list is on the next page.

EMPLOYABILITY TRAITS CHECKLIST

Employability trait	Got it	Need to work on it
1. Communication		
a. reading	_____	_____
b. writing	_____	_____
c. speaking	_____	_____
d. listening	_____	_____
2. Math	_____	_____
3. Ability and experience with computers	_____	_____
4. Ability to work in a team	_____	_____
5. Attendance, attendance, attendance	_____	_____
6. Willingness to learn	_____	_____
7. A positive attitude	_____	_____
8. Independence	_____	_____
9. Flexibility	_____	_____

Employability trait (cont.)	Got it	Need to work on it
10. Ability to organize and prioritize	------ ------ ------	------ ------ ------
11. Leadership	------	------
12. Problem solving	------	------
13. Confidence	------	------
14. Overall skills	------	------

List any and all other "can-dos" you currently have

List any other "can do's" you'll need

PARENT TO PARENT

"My advice to other parents is to first consider your teenager and his or her needs, and then to remember that you are dealing with a young adult. We can attempt to set limits during adolescence on issues such as curfews, drinking, friendships, etc., but values and decision-making have been instilled in earlier years. Recognizing how important communication is, and how little our teenagers tend to share with us, I would concentrate on "listening to them" to determine how you can best approach this passage in their lives. S/he may not have the big picture, or the wisdom and experience of an adult, but the decision is one with which s/he must be comfortable and must "own". And there is rarely only one right answer, so the more important lesson here might be that we support our children's decision-making and their choices."

WHERE TO GET WHAT EMPLOYERS WANT

DEGREES

Many careers require your child to get a degree from an institution of higher learning after high school. If this is the case, your child will need to begin examining some of these schools starting in his/her junior year. What schools you will look into will be determined by the degree that the career requires. If your child's choice requires a bachelor's degree, you will need to examine four year colleges and universities. If your child's choice requires an associate degree, you will look at junior colleges, career and technology schools, and community colleges.

The following section will be dedicated to the process of examining and selecting one of these educational opportunities. The investment in time and money is well worth it. According to the U.S. Department of Commerce, those workers without a high school diploma will average only $14, 162 annually; those with a high school diploma will average $21,430; those with an associate degree will average $27,780; and those workers with a bachelor's degree will average $36,979. The number of years worked also diminishes significantly with increased education.

COLLEGES AND UNIVERSITIES

If the career that your child wants to pursue requires a bachelor's degree, he/she will need to graduate from a four-year college or university. If you are wondering what the difference is between colleges and universities, let me explain. Four-year colleges offer bachelor's and associate degrees. Colleges tend to be smaller than universities and usually do not have graduate schools offering advanced degrees. Universities, on the other hand, consist of several colleges and do offer masters and doctoral degrees. There are over 1600 colleges and universities in this country, and together they make up the best system of higher education in the world.

Four-year colleges and universities have received some criticism as of late for not preparing people for the work world, but that criticism is not entirely deserved. In many cases when you find people who have graduated from a four-year college or university and find themselves unemployable, it is because they have not used their four-year education correctly. Every four-year institution has a long list of majors that students can study. Some of those majors are the kind that you want for your child. These majors will be the ones that specifically prepare your child to market him/herself by saying, "Here is what I am, and here is what I can do". Examples would be computer programming, nursing, and engineering. Others majors are the kind where you just study a subject. Picking one of these majors will leave a student far less employable.

You will find many careers that require you to get a bachelor's degree in a specific major. If your child's career requires this, you will need to find out just what colleges are out there and what they have to offer. There are two ways to do this.

College Fairs- Most high schools will have college fairs once a year. Attending one of these during your child's sophomore or junior year in high school will allow you to gather information about a number of colleges that are in your area.

College Guides- You will find a number of college guides in your local public library, high school guidance office, and bookstores. These guides list just about every accredited four-year college in the country. They also give you detailed information about each of these schools. The following is a list of such guides.

<u>Peterson's Guide to Four-Year Colleges</u>
<u>Barron's Profile of American Colleges</u>
<u>ARCO, The Right College</u>
<u>The College Handbook-College Board</u>
<u>Lovejoy's College Guide</u>
<u>The College Blue Book</u>
<u>Cass & Birnbaum Guide to American Colleges</u>

If you are sure that your child will be pursuing a four-year degree, you should keep one of these at the house. Under every college listing you will find information about student life, housing, sports, programs of study, graduation requirements, graduation rates, tuition, financial aid, and admissions requirements. These are great books and are packed with information and advise about selecting four-year colleges, and you want as much information as you can get on as many colleges as you can find.

To start your search you will need to find about five colleges that award the specific degree that your child requires. List these five colleges on the appropriate sheet in your career folder and turn to the next section of this book entitled "CHECKING OUT SCHOOLS".

One option for getting an associate degree that has been growing in popularity recently is the career school. This is a general name for a technical, trade, or business school. These schools are usually private schools that offer very specific training directly related to a single career. Many offer associate degrees, while others offer certificates of completion. If the career that interests your child requires an associate degree, make sure that the technical school you are examining will offer the associate degree. Some will -- others will not.

When your child attends one of these schools, he/she usually enters a program that is designated for a specific career. The study in many of these programs is also limited to that one specific career. For example, if your child enters a program that will train him/her to be a computer aided drafter, all or most of his/her classes will be directly related to being a computer aided drafter. This is in sharp contrast to four-year colleges that will also require your child to study things such as English Literature, Philosophy, Psychology, etc.

Using a career school can be a major advantage for some students, especially if they have struggled with some of these other courses in high school. I have run across countless examples of students who were tremendously successful at career schools but were not so successful in their overall academic achievement in high school. These students may have succeeded in one or two classes that interested them at the high school level but fell behind in the other classes. The career school approach is ideal for this student because during his/her time at that career school, he/she will be studying primarily those subjects that interest him/her.

The Career School can also benefit the student who really does not like school but realizes that he/she needs some more education to get into his/her chosen career field. Because the courses are limited to the ones that are required to qualify for a specific career, the time required is significantly shorter than the time required to finish a four-year college. This fact is backed up by a 1996 study by the U.S. Department of Education called <u>Nontraditional Undergraduates.</u> It stated that students who were considered "high risk", and had entered a certification program for the first time in 1989-90, had a far greater success rate than those "high risk" students who entered an associate or bachelor's degree program.

Please don't misunderstand. The career school option is great even for very strong students as long as the career that interests them can be reached through this approach. The following is a list of careers offered at various career schools throughout the country. If your child's career interests match with one or more of these you may wish to consider this option.

Accounting
Accounting and Automation
Administrative Assistant
Advertising Writer/Artist
Air Conditioning/Refrigeration/Heating
Airframe and Power Plant Technology
Airline/Travel - Computer Reservations
Allied Health
Appliance Repair
Architectural and Computer-Aided Design
Artist - Commercial
Artist - Fine
Auto Body Paint & Mechanical Technology
Auto Body Repair
Automotive Service Technology - Basic and Certified
Automotive Technician
Aviation Maintenance Technician
Baking and Pastry Arts
Bank Teller
Barbering/ Hair Stylist
Blueprint Reader
Broadcaster
Building Maintenance Technician
Business Administration - Accounting and Management
Business Analysis

Business Information Processor
Cardiac Technician/ Cardiovascular Technology
Computer Aided Drafting
Computer Animation
Computer Engineering Technology
Computer Installation and Repair
Computer Laboratory Technician
Computer Maintenance Technology
Computer Operations
Computer Programming
Computer Technology and Information
Cosmetology
Court Reporting
Criminal Justice
Culinary Arts
Data Entry/ Data Processor
Dental Assistant
Desktop Publishing
Diesel Mechanic
Diesel Technology
Digital Electronics
Diver, Commercial/Inspection/NDT
Drafting
ECG/EKG Technician
Electrician
Electronic Assembly Technology
Electronic Engineering Technology
Electronics Specialist
Electronics Technician
Emergency Medical Technician
Equine Studies
Esthetics
Executive Assistant
Executive Secretary
Fashion Design
Fashion Illustrator
Fashion Merchandising
Film/Video/Photography
Financial Administration Assistant
Food and Beverage Management

Food Service Specialist
General Business
General Office
Graphic Design
Graphic Illustration
Hair Styling
Health Claims Examiner
Heating Mechanic
Heating, Ventilation, Air Conditioning
Home Health Aide
Home Health Medical Aide
Hospitality Management
Hotel and Restaurant management
Hotel/Motel Management
Human Anatomy and Physiology
Illustrator
Instrumentation Specialist
Insurance
Insurance Coding Specialist
Insurance Processor
Interior Design
Laboratory Technician
Legal Administrative Assistant
Legal Assistant Paralegal
Legal Secretary
Locksmith
Loss Prevention Security Officer
Management
Manicuring
Marine Technology
Marketing
Mechanical/Electrical/Drafting/ Design
Medical Assistant
Medical Coding
Medical Laboratory Technician
Medical Office Manager
Medical Records Technician
Medical Secretary
Medical Transcriptionist
Medical/Dental Administrative Assistant

Medical/Dental Receptionist
Motion Picture/Television Production
Multimedia
Netware Administrator
Netware Engineer
Nurse's Aide
Nursing
Nursing Assistant
Occupational Therapy Assistant
Office Automation Technology
Office Machine Repair
Office Technology
Optometric Assistant
Paralegal
Pharmacy Assistant
Pharmacy Technician Assistant
Phlebotomist
Photographer
Physical Therapy Assistant
Plumber
Printer
Programmer Analyst
Psychiatric Technology
Publishing/Graphic Arts/Desktop Production
Radio and Television Broadcasting
Receptionist
Recording Specialist
Respiratory Specialist
Restaurant Management
Retailer
Sales
Secretary Transcriptionist
Sign Language Interpreter
Skin Care Specialist
Sports Operations and Management
Surgical Technician
Surveyor
Teacher Education, Business
Telecommunications
Tool and Die Designer

Travel and Tourism
Travel Specialist
Truck Technology
Veterinary Assistant
Vocational Nurse
Welding
Word Processing
X-Ray Technician

You can get information about career schools in much the same way as you get information about colleges.

College Fairs- Career schools will participate in the same college fairs as the four-year colleges. Because of the specialized nature of career schools, you will usually have less choices for your particular specialty than with colleges

College Guides- There are books listing all associate degree schools, including career schools, in your local libraries, guidance offices, and bookstores that are similar to the guides for four-year colleges. In many cases these guides will be published by the same companies.

Career College Association- If you still cannot find enough information from these sources, you can write to the Career College Association and ask for the <u>Handbook of Accredited Private Trade and Technical Schools</u>. The address is, 750 1st St., NE., Washington, DC 20002.

Career Training Foundation- The Career Training Foundation also has a book called the <u>Guide to Careers in America</u>. It is a great resource for anyone considering career schools. The book includes information on nearly all of the career schools in the country, as well as some other helpful hints about the career school approach. The Career Training Foundation can be contacted at: 750 First Street, NE, Suite 900, Washington, DC 20002. Their phone number is (202) 336-6800. They also have a web site that is in conjunction with the Career College Association (www.career.org).

After finding several career schools that offer the specific associate's degree that your child's career choices require turn to the section of this chapter titled "CHECKING OUT SCHOOLS".

COMMUNITY COLLEGES

Another way to get an associate degree will be at your local community college. According to the American Association of Community Colleges there are 1,123 community colleges in the country. These community colleges enroll more than 5 billion students annually. Community colleges offer a wide variety of courses, and those courses can usually be taken at the student's leisure. This is probably one of the biggest advantages to using this option. Instead of having to enroll in a school's program that requires you to take a "package" of classes, you can instead design your own schedule. In fact, according to the AACC, 64 percent of their students are enrolled part-time. You will, however, have to take a predetermined set of courses to get the associate degree.

Another advantage of checking with your local community college is that you can save a great deal of money. Again, I encourage you to leave the money out of the decision until later, but when talking about advantages of community colleges, you have to talk about money.

You will save in two ways. First, the cost of community colleges is usually far less than any other school. According to the AACC the average annual cost for tuition and fees is only $1,518. Second, because community colleges are usually close to where you live, your child will again save several thousand dollars per year on room and board. You will have to consider the cost of a car, insurance, maintenance, and gas.

Community colleges can be used to prepare for colleges, and many students use them for this very purpose. Going to a community college for your first two years of college can save significant amounts of tuition. However, special care must be taken to ensure that the credits will transfer to the four-year college of your child's choice. The best way to determine this is to inquire at the four-year college that your child wants to attend.

Many students use the community college as an end in itself. If the career that your child chose requires an associate degree or a specific certificate, most community colleges should be able to provide these qualifications. According to the AACC, 500,000 associate's degrees are awarded annually as well as 300,000 two-year certificates.

As the work force becomes more specialized the demand for community college and other two-year-program graduates has increased. These graduates are finding their incomes climbing along with the demand. A graduate from a community college or other two year program can expect to earn $250,000 more over their lifetime than the average high school graduate. The AACC reports that the average annual income for community college graduates over the last three years has gone from $20,753 to $25,771. This is an increase of more than 24%.

Community colleges will never be as famous as their four-year counterparts. Lacking the research facilities, hospitals, and sports teams that most universities have, they get very little publicity. Despite their lack of clout, community colleges have served as the first step for many famous people. NASA Space Shuttle Commander, - Lieutenant Colonel Eileen Collins, NAACP President, - Kweisi Mfume, and Baseball Superstar, - Nolan Ryan all got their start at community colleges.

You can get information about community colleges by using the exact same methods described in the career school section. Also, because they are local, you will find their number in the phone book. Use the questions in CHECKING OUT SCHOOLS to evaluate your local community college. If you are on the web, the American Association of Community Colleges has a great site filled with information. See www.acc.nche.edu/

JUNIOR COLLEGES

The last option for picking up the associate degree that we will examine will be the junior college. Many people think of junior colleges as just stepping stones for moving on to four-year colleges. While they can be used this way, the junior college can also be used as an end. Junior colleges will be very similar in their approach as the four-year colleges, but instead of offering the bachelor's degree they offer the associate degree.

They will be different from technical schools in that the courses may include things like English and History in addition to the classes relating to the career that your child will be pursuing.

You can find out about junior colleges in the exact same way you would find out about career school.

POST GRADUATE DEGREES

If the career that your child has selected will require them to get a master's, doctoral, or professional degree, turn to the section at the end of this chapter on post graduate degrees. This option will require some special consideration, and to cover this degree here could be confusing.

CHECKING OUT SCHOOLS

After you have found several schools that will award the degree that is required by your child's career, you will need to see if these schools are right for your child in other ways. The best way to do this would actually be to visit the schools. Many schools will have specific days for group visitation, others will allow you to visit and tour the school on an individual basis whenever it is convenient for you.

VISITING THE SCHOOLS

Visiting schools should be done in the second semester of your child's junior year, the following summer, or very early in his/her senior year. A visit can be arranged by contacting someone in the admissions office. You can visit schools almost any day of the week, but it is sometimes best to visit during a weekday and during the morning or afternoon hours. Visiting at this time will allow you and your child to actually see the school during working hours. You will have the opportunity to see classes in progress and even talk to students.

You may need to take a vacation day to do this, but it will be worth it. If you are worried about your child being marked absent from class, call the guidance office. Many high schools will have several "visitation days" that your child can use. These days are set aside for this very purpose and your child will not be counted as absent.

When visiting the college there are several things that you need to find out. As you get answers for each of the following questions make notes on your career sheet. You may also wish to take pictures of the campus as a reminder.

Below are listed some questions that you may wish to ask. Write these questions on your career sheet ahead of time as well as any other questions that you may wish to have answered. This will prevent you from forgetting anything and will also help to keep you focused. You may wish to encourage your child to ask his/her own questions. This will keep the discussion focused on your child and will also give a better impression to the person doing the tour.

Don't be intimidated by this process. Many people feel that the decision is solely up to the college or school whether or not your child is allowed to attend. The truth is that it is primarily your decision, especially at this point of the game. On this visit you and your child are deciding if this school is good enough for you, not if your child is good enough for this school!

IMPORTANT QUESTIONS TO ASK WHILE VISITING

The questions that are the most important and should be answered immediately should sound something like this:

1. "I would like to become a _____. When I graduate from here will I be one?"

This is the most important question. As I have stressed all along, in order for your child to be "marketable", he/she will need to approach a personnel director and tell that person exactly what he/she is and exactly what he/she can do. Your child will not make the mistake of spending four years studying just a subject, but instead will be studying and preparing for a specific career.

2. "What licenses or certifications will I have when I graduate? Will I need any licenses or certifications to do this job?"

This can provide more assurance that you will be prepared for a specific career.

3. "Have people who have graduated with this major had any trouble finding employment? What are some of your recent graduates in this major doing now?"

Remember that this is why you are here, to prepare yourself to be employed in a specific career, not just to be educated about that career.

4. "Do you have placement assistance? What is your placement rate?"

Many colleges and schools offer placement assistance. This can range from something as simple as giving students lists of potential employers to something much more sophisticated. The best placement departments will be ones that actually assist your child by contacting employers and helping to arrange interviews. I don't know of any school that can guarantee your child a job upon completion of his/her program, but the better schools will have

105

the higher placement rates. To make sure that these rates are telling you exactly what you want to know, you may wish to ask, "What percent of last years graduates are working in the field for which they trained?" You may also wish to visit the placement center and see how things are done.

5. "Where are these people being hired? Are there opportunities locally or will I have to relocate?"

This again is one of those questions that has to be answered. If the opportunities are not local, then consideration will have to be given about how seriously your child wants to relocate.

6. "I want to get some experience in the field before I graduate. Do you have an established internship program?"

Internships are a must. Trying to get a job without any experience is an up-hill battle. Make sure that the schools you are are examining have internships available.

MORE QUESTIONS

Now that you know this school can train your child for his/her particular career choice, you will need to see if this school will be an academic match for your child. What you want to determine now is whether or not your child will be able to perform to a level that will allow him or her to graduate. This is a very important point, especially considering the number of students that start colleges and schools but do not finish. During this part of the process it is very important that you be completely honest with yourself. Some training requires certain aptitudes, and if your child just happens to lack those aptitudes, then continuing down this path will probably lead to frustration and failure.

Ask the following questions, and again be sure to jot down the answers on your career sheet.

7. "Do you require SAT or ACT scores?"

Most colleges will require some sort of standardized test scores. Many of the associate degree training options will not require these tests. You will need to know this so that you can schedule a time for your son or daughter to take these tests. Most high schools offer these tests at their own facilities or at a neighboring school. If your child has not yet been told when and where these tests are, call the guidance counselor at his/her school. The SAT test is the most commonly used test and should be taken as many times as possible. Usually taking it two or three times starting in the second semester of their junior year will be sufficient. There is a small fee for taking this test, but if you think you will have trouble paying for it there is a form you can fill out which may allow you to have the fee waved.

8. "What is the minimum test score required for entrance?"

Many colleges will set a minimum score for admission to their school. This number is used as an indicator of your child's ability to succeed. If your child's score turns out to be lower than that score, chances are that he/she may not be admitted to the school.

9. "What is the range for SAT scores of your students? What is the range of SAT scores for the students in my particular field of study?"

This will tell your child how he/she will rank among the other students. It is a very valuable piece of information. If your child's scores are near the top, you can feel assured that his/her ability to handle the academic load is pretty good. If his/her score is near the bottom of the range, then your child needs to know that the academic load will be challenging. He/she can do it, but his/her level of commitment and excitement for the career they are training for must be high enough to drive him/her through the challenges.

10. "Do you require a certain grade point average?"

This again you will need to know in order to see if your child has a chance for being accepted to that school. It can also be used to partially gauge of your child's chances of success.

11. "What classes have to be taken in high school?"

Many degree programs in higher education require that you have completed certain levels of math or have completed certain other subjects before you enroll in that major. If your child has not yet taken these courses, you will have to make arrangements for him/her to take these courses during the next school year or even during the summer. If your local high school does not offer these courses in a fashion that would be convenient for your child's completion check and see what courses at your local community college could be substituted.

12. "What is your graduation rate?"

This is a great question for finding out what your child's chances are to finish at this particular school. Some schools have tremendous support systems for their students and pride themselves on graduating a high percentage of their students.

OK, after asking these questions you should have a pretty good idea about where your child stands academically, and what his/her chances are of finishing that particular program of study. If you have determined that your child fits into the ranges given and can fulfill the demands for entrance, then you know that this is still one of your choices. If your child does not seem to fit into the requirements of the school, or has a lower grade point average or standardized test score, you might wish to look elsewhere.

Many parents want to push the limit here and try to get their child into a school that might just be too difficult for him/her. This can be a huge mistake. Right away the odds will be stacked against your child. Colleges and even some associate degree programs can be very competitive, and if your child is not prepared because of academic ability or lack of interest, they will not be able to keep up with a campus full of academically stronger students. If you do push them into this sort of situation, don't change their bedroom into an office or den because they will be back.

Please don't let this be an insult or setback. If you believe that your child might not be able to handle the academic load of a particular school you may actually be ahead of the game. It is much easier to admit this now instead of having your child suffer through the stress and financial loss of withdrawing from a school.

Now, if you have come to the realization that this particular college or school might be too difficult, simply move on to another. If this happens at several colleges, you may wish to look into other training options. Remember, though, that the training options that you look into must be able to get your child to the career goal that he/she had selected earlier. If the only way to get there is by using a college, in other words the particular goal selected by your child requires a four-year or two-year degree, then you are forced to do some soul searching with your child.

Simply sit down with your child and lay all the cards on the table. Say something like this, " I know you said that you wanted to be a --------------, but that would require you completing a four-year college or this particular associate's degree program. With your grades and test scores you might find things a bit difficult. Do you think that your desire to be a ---------------- is strong enough that you will be able to stick it out for__?__years?" If your child's desire or interest fades, you may wish to look at some of the other career goals that you had established earlier. If your child's heart seems set on this career, drop your doubts right away! Gather up as much enthusiasm as you can muster and get behind them!

You may find that if the enthusiasm your child has for this career is strong enough, he/she can overcome all kinds of obstacles. I firmly believe that this is one of the advantages of having selected a specific career goal before starting this part of the process. Your child now sees "why" he/she is going to school and what the end result of his/her efforts will be. In fact, don't be

109

surprised if his/her academic performance in high school picks up after selecting a specific goal.

If you are in a situation where you and your child are looking at a school that requires a higher grade point average or test scores than your child has, there are ways to deal with this. First contact your guidance counselor and ask if courses that your child may have scored low on can be taken over in the summer to erase those earlier bad grades. Also ask what SAT or other test preparation is available. Using a formal SAT test preparation program such as the Kaplan course can have some benefit on your child's test score. To contact someone at Kaplan call

1-800-KAP-ITEMS.

You can also find books and software that can be very helpful.

Now that we are continuing on and keeping a particular school as one of our options, we need to see if this school is a match in other ways.

TAKE A TOUR

The best thing to do here is just walk around. Ask for a tour of the campus and its facilities. When taking this tour you simply want your child to see as much of the campus and as many of the students as possible. This part of the process is a little less scientific, but no less important. You want an environment that will be comfortable for your child.

You may at this point allow your child to tour the campus without you, preferably with a current student. This will free your child to be more him/herself and will also allow him/her to see things from a student's perspective.

You and your child should be looking for a number of different things. When walking by the classrooms look inside and see if the students are are interested in what they are doing. You will also want to take a look at the equipment (laboratory equipment, computers, library materials) available to your child

110

to make sure that he/she will not be learning on out-dated relics. If you don't know what equipment is necessary, make sure that you ask someone in the admissions department if the equipment is modern and equivalent to what is being used in the work force.

While your child is taking the tour, take one of your own. While on your tour, take pictures of the campus and also take notes so you can review them later with your child. Make sure that you and your child see as much as possible, including dorms and classes in progress.

When you have completed your tour, ask for an application. Also ask about the school's specific requirements such as deadlines for applying and acceptance criterion.

The drive home will be a very enlightening experience.

THE DRIVE HOME

This is a great opportunity for some quality time with your child. At this point ask him/her some questions about what he/she thought. Try and reserve judgment until a later time. If your child knows that you disapprove of something, he/she may be less likely to be open with you about that subject.

By the time you get home have the following questions answered:

1)   What was your overall impression?

2)   What did you think of the academic requirements... do you think you could do well at this school?

3)   What about the location? Will you feel comfortable "in the city" or "in the middle of nowhere?"

4)   What did you think about the other students? Do you think you can fit-in here?

5)   What were the dorms like? If you choose to live on

campus, would you feel comfortable with those living arrangements?

6) What did you think of the classes ?

7) With all things considered, is this one of your options that you would like to keep open?

8) Are you still excited about being a (career choice)?

9) Do you have any concerns? Is there anything that you did not like about this school?

When you get home make sure that you record all of the answers to these questions on your career sheet.

IF:
     ... the response to this school was favorable,
     ... your child is still excited about their particular career
         choice,
     ... this school will train your child for their particular
         career choice , and
     ...your child seems to meet the academic requirements
         of that school,

YOU ARE WELL ON YOUR WAY TO HELPING YOUR CHILD MAKE THIS CHOICE.

PARENT TO PARENT

"Our oldest son hated school and wanted nothing to do with college. He joined the army when he was seventeen and left home a month after graduating high school. We were very concerned about his future but there was no talking to him..........Seventeen years later he is still in the army, was twice recognized as Soldier of the Year in regional competitions, owns his own business (a grocery store) and is the proud father of a twelve year old who is so academically advanced that he is already being asked to take the SAT test . Wow!"

WHERE TO GET WHAT EMPLOYERS WANT

SPECIALIZED TRAINING

Many careers will not require a degree, but will require specialized training beyond high school. This specialized training can be received by the same institutions where you would receive degrees, but can also be picked up elsewhere. Let's look at two of these other options.

THE MILITARY

This is one training option that is overlooked by a great number of parents. The main reason is that most parents just don't realize how many different specialties exist in the military. Some believe that the military trains for one thing and one thing only, and that is "how to fight a war". The truth of the matter is that the military is filled with support personnel in just about every career field imaginable. Including positions occupied by officers, there are over 150 different careers fields. Each of those careers fields offers continuing education and training (over 300 training programs with over 10,000 courses), and most will have civilian counterparts.

Many people have had children go into the military after high school, but in many of the cases their child went in that direction because that child just did not want to go to school or had no clue what he/she wanted to do and were just buying time. The military can be used to allow your child some time to mature and to gain access to government benefits, but why not also use this option to prepare for a specific career.

One major factor that has kept many parents from encouraging their children to examine the military option is the risk that he/she might be called on in times of war or international tension to serve in a situation that would be very dangerous. Sure, this is a consideration, but if your child chooses a field that is one of the specialties that will allow him/her to train for a career in civilian life, he/she probably won't be on the "front line".

Another factor that has limited parents from examining this training option is the misconception that the military is just for those people who are not academically strong enough to go to a post-secondary school. Nothing could be further from the truth. In fact, the selection criteria for the military has become a great deal more difficult. Some branches of the military are even going into the high schools and actively seeking out some of the stronger students for their specialized programs. A great example would be the Navy's nuclear program.

One other thing to consider is that the military has incredible financial packages that can help your child pay for additional education when he/she leaves the service. Students can qualify for the Montgomery GI Bill after only one tour. They will then have access to up to $15,835 dollars for education. Even joining the Reserve or the National Guard can qualify students for up to $7,523. (These benefits are subject to change.) If your child qualifies for military college funds, the total educational assistance can increase up to $40,000. All of this while earning just under $1000 per month salary.

If your child is willing to keep this option open and does not mind the extra responsibilities that go along with a short stint in the military, I would encourage you to further examine this option. Even if your sources did not recommend this as one of your options, it would not hurt to investigate what the military has to offer. Remember that there are several branches of the military. Opportunities are available in the Army, Navy, Air Force, Marine Corps, and the Coast Guard as well as the reserve units for these branches and the National Guard. One branch might offer specialties that another does not, so you would be well advised to examine them all.

CALL THE RECRUITER

One of the first things that you will want to do is call your local recruiters. Their phone numbers are in the phone book under US Government. You may also have the opportunity to talk to recruiters at one of the college fairs at your local high school.

The first thing that you need to do is to tell the recruiters what the specific career is that your child is interested in pursuing. Ask them if they can train someone for that career in their particular branch of the service. If the answers are favorable, you may wish to investigate this option further. Simply set up a time when you and your child can sit down together and ask a few questions of the recruiter.

One thing that your child will need to do in order to qualify

117

for military enlistment is take the Armed Forces Vocational Aptitude Battery (ASVAB). This battery of tests evaluates abilities and aptitudes that will apply to various specialties within the military. In order to qualify for the specialty of choice, your child will need to perform well. Your child can take this test at your local Military Entrance Processing Station or at your local high school.

CAREERS YOUR CHILD CAN TRAIN FOR USING THE MILITARY

There are 8 different career training categories for enlisted personnel in the military. The following is a list of those categories as well as the specific careers included in those categories. More careers are available, but only after acquiring college degrees.

Compare the careers that interest your child with the ones offered. If the military offers training in your child's chosen career, you may wish to examine the military option more closely. If your child's career choice is not included, look for something that is comparable or move on to other training options.

Human services

Caseworkers and Counselors
Religious Program Specialists

Media and Public Affairs

Photographic Specialists
Interpreters and Translators
Musicians
Audiovisual and Broadcast Technicians
Broadcast Journalists and News writers
Graphic Designers and Illustrators

Health Care

Radiologic (x-ray) technicians
Cardiopulmonary and EEG Technicians
Pharmacy Technicians
Dental Specialists
Physical and Occupational Therapy Specialists
Medical Laboratory Technicians
Medical Records Technicians
Medical Service Technicians
Optometric Technicians

Engineering, Science, and Technical

Communications Equipment Operators
Space Operations Specialists
Ordinance Specialists
Air Traffic Controllers
Radar and Sonar Operators
Meteorological Specialists
Chemical Laboratory Specialists
Radio Intelligence Specialists
Non-Destructive Testers
Computer Programmers
Emergency Management Specialists
Environmental Health and Safety Specialists
Intelligence Specialists
Surveying, Mapping, and Drafting Technicians

Administrative

Recruiting Specialist
Personnel Specialist
Postal Specialist
Flight Operations Specialists
Preventive Maintenance Analysts
Legal Specialists and Court Reporters
Administrative Support Specialists
Computer Systems Specialists
Finance and Accounting Specialists

119

Sales and Stock Specialists
Supply and Warehousing Specialists
Training Specialists and Instructors
Transportation Specialists

Service

Law Enforcement and Security Specialists
Military Police
Firefighters
Food Service Specialists

Vehicle and Machinery Mechanic

Aircraft Mechanics
Automotive and Heavy Equipment Mechanics
Divers
Heating and Cooling Mechanics
Marine Engine Mechanics
Powerhouse Mechanics

Electric and Electrical Equipment Repair

Computer Equipment Repairers
Electrical Products Repairers
Weapons Maintenance Technicians
Aircraft Electricians
Electronic Instrument Repairers
Communications Equipment Repairers
Photographic Equipment Repairers
Power Plant Electricians
Precision Instrument Repairers
Radar and Sonar Equipment Repairers
Ship Electricians

Construction

Construction Equipment Operators
Construction Specialists
Plumbers and Pipe Fitters
Building Electricians

Machine Operator and Precision Work

Welders and Metal Workers
Survival Equipment Specialists
Water and Sewage Treatment Plant Operators
Compressed Gas Technicians
Dental and Optical Laboratory Technicians
Machinist
Power Plant Operators
Printing Specialists

Transportation and Materials Handling

Air Crew Members Vehicle Drivers
Aircraft Launch and Recovery Specialists
Cargo Specialists
Flight Engineers
Petroleum Supply Specialists
Quartermasters and Boat Operators
Seamen

Combat Specialty

Combat Engineers
Infantrymen
Special Operations Forces
Artillery Crew Members
Tank Crew Members

For detailed details on these careers call your local recruiter or go to www.military careers.com. You can also call toll free to the following:

Army   (800) USA-ARMY
Navy   (800) USA-NAVY
Air Force   (800) 423-USAF
Marine Corps   (800) MARINES
Coast Guard   (800) 424-8883
Air National Guard   (800) TO GO ANG
Army National Guard   (800) GO GUARD

Here are some of the things that you may wish to ask as you work with your local recruiter.

1. **"My child wants to be a _____, can he/she train for this career in your branch of the military?"**

Again, we must keep asking this question.

2. **"When my child finishes his/her time in the military will he/she then be employable in the civilian market as a _____."**

This is a very important point. What your child will do in the military, and what he/she will be qualified to do in civilian life can sometimes be different. What you want to determine is whether or not your child will receive certain licenses or certifications that are recognized in the the civilian work place.

3. **"Is this specialty training going to be guaranteed for my child?"**

The only acceptable answer here is, yes! You have to make sure that the years your son or daughter will spend in the military will be productive years that will lead him/her in the direction that he/she wants to go. If the training is not guaranteed your child might find him/herself in a specialty that has nothing to do with what he/she wants to be.

4. **"What are your requirements for being accepted into this specialty?"**

This is not a question that most parents expect to ask when dealing with the military. With today's high-tech specialties, however, the military has had to be much more selective in whom they recruit. You will find that with some specialties the military can be just as selective as a four-year college.

123

5. **"What classes will my child need to take in high school?"**

6. **"How much time will they have to commit to the military in order to receive this training?"**

You will need to find out about two things here. How much "active duty" time will be required, that is, how much time will he/she be a full-time soldier. And, how much "reserve time" will be required. This cannot be overlooked. Your child may not be required to serve as an active reservist who attends meetings, but he/she may be required to serve as an inactive reservist. As a member of the inactive reserve, your child won't be required to attend meetings and won't be paid, but in the case of a National Emergency he/she could be "called up" for active duty. This actually happened during the Gulf War. I'm sure that a number of former military personnel were surprised to know that this could happen.

7. **"How much time will I have to spend in "Basic Training"? How difficult is "Basic Training"?"**

This has to be taken into consideration. Granted, basic training is not quite as physically demanding as it used to be, but it is still difficult and unpleasant. Most healthy young adults should be able to handle the physical part. The mental part can be somewhat of a problem. As long as your child can handle being away from the comforts of home and can deal with a "less than pleasant" drill instructor, he/she should be fine. This needs to be addressed, however, in order to make sure that your child will be able to finish the process that he/she started.

8. **"What benefits will I receive that I can use when I leave the military?"**

This is the question that your recruiter will love you for asking. The military has tremendous benefits for people who want to continue their education. Not only will your child get specialized training while serving, but he/she will have the opportunity to take courses in civilian schools during his/her service and will have a number of benefits for paying for an education after he/she has served.

These questions should be sufficient in order for you and your child to decide if you want to continue to consider this training option. If your child is excited about the idea there is one more thing that you might want to do.

ASK SOMEONE WHO HAS BEEN THERE

Ask your recruiter to arrange an opportunity for your child to meet with someone from a local reserve unit who was trained in the specialty that your child has selected. This is absolutely invaluable. If you must, push the issue. You may have to travel to the reserve unit that has a person with this specialty, but it will be worth it. Chances are that your recruiter will know " a little about a lot". A person who is actually in that specialty, however, will know "a lot about a little", in particular - your child's specialty. This person will also be less inclined to push the military option since they don't have an interest in your child going into the military.

If you do get the opportunity to do speak to someone in the military who is not a recruiter, here are some questions that you may wish to ask;

1.   "Did your training in this specialty prepare you for the same career in civilian life?"

2.   "How long did you work in the field? Are you in the field now?"

3.   "Was the training very difficult to complete?"

4.   "Would you recommend this as a training option to get into this career?"

You will come up with other questions as you talk with this person, but the ones that I just gave you will be the most

125

important ones.

THE DRIVE HOME

After you have had the opportunity to speak with the representatives from the military, you need to review some things with your child.

1.   "Do you still want to be a _____?"

2.   "Are you satisfied that you can get to your career goal by using the military?"

3.   "Are you willing to make the sacrifices required by the military to get the training you need?"

4.   "Do you think you will finish?"

APPRENTICESHIPS

An apprenticeship is an opportunity for your child to learn a skill or a trade while working with someone who is experienced in the field. Certain careers will require this form of training exclusively. While working with this person, a journeyman, your child will learn by directly observing and by gradually being assigned the tasks that your child will be doing upon completion. There will also be some classroom instruction that has been designed by a cooperation between the Bureau of Apprenticeship Training and the sponsors of these apprenticeships. The sponsors of these apprenticeships are the companies or labor unions who actually employ people with these skills. The time requirement is anywhere from one to six years, and the average is about four years. At the completion of the program your child will be a journeyman and will then be able to market him/herself as such.

It is amazing that so little is known about this option, especially considering that you can train for over 830 careers using apprenticeships. More than half of these careers are in the construction field, one of the few manufacturing fields expected to increase it's demands for new hires. Others range from fire fighters to legal secretaries, and new apprenticeships are being developed with industry demand.

Like some of the other training options that are available, there is some competition involved in applying for admission to an apprenticeship program. The requirements will vary depending on the program. Most apprenticeships will require a high school diploma or better, as well as strong math and communication skills. It also helps if your child has had the opportunity to take related courses at his/her high school or local vocational technical school.

One of the advantages of using an apprenticeship is that you don't have to pay tuition. You may be required to pay for books, supplies and union dues, but those should be your child's only expenses. Your child should be able to pay for these on his/her own because while he/she is being trained they will also be paid. The pay your child receives will be far less than he/she will make

127

at the end of his/her training, but it will help pay the bills.

Another advantage is that apprenticeships are limited to industry demand. In other words, if the demand is low for a certain specialty there will be few openings. You may be wondering why this is an advantage. Well, why should your child invest several years training for a career if he/she won't be able to find employment afterwards.

Exploring the apprenticeship option is facilitated by some programs in high schools and technical schools. These programs acquaint children with the opportunities in crafts and trades and give them theoretical and technical instruction in the specific fields.

Some apprenticeship programs may even have pre-job programs. Pre-job programs provide on-the-job training for 6 to 8 weeks. Their purpose is to introduce potential apprentices to specific skilled trades and to help the potential apprentice to determine his/her suitability to the trade. When a student successfully finishes this pre-job program he/she may continue in the actual apprenticeship.

Apprenticeships will probably continue to grow in popularity and availability as the demand for skilled workers also grows. The growth from 1980 to 1990 indicates this trend. During that time period the demand for skilled workers and specific craft oriented employees skyrocketed from 11 million to 14 million.

GETTING STARTED

Before beginning an apprenticeship program your child will need to determine if the career he/she has selected can be reached using an apprenticeship. To obtain a complete list of the over 800 careers that you can prepare for using apprenticeship programs, or to get help finding apprentice programs, contact your local Bureau of Apprenticeship Training State Offices and Apprenticeship Councils. The phone numbers for these agencies are provided below. Following this list I have included another list that details the apprenticeships that are the most popular and available.

ALABAMA	(205) 731-1308
ALASKA	(271) 271-5035
ARIZONA	(602) 252-7771
ARKANSAS	(501) 378-5415
CALIFORNIA	(415) 737-2700
COLORADO	(303) 844-4793
CONNECTICUT	(203) 566-4724
DELAWARE	(302) 571-1908
DISTRICT OF COLUMBIA	(202) 639-1415
FLORIDA	(904) 488-8332
GEORGIA	(404) 347-4403
HAWAII	(808) 548-2520
IDAHO	(208) 334-1013
ILLINOIS	(312) 353-4690
INDIANA	(317) 269-7592
IOWA	(515) 284-4690
KANSAS	(913) 296-3588
KENTUCKY	(502) 588-5223
LOUISIANA	(504) 342-7820
MAINE	(207) 289-4307
MARYLAND	(301) 333-5718
MASSACHUSETTS	(617) 727-3488
MICHIGAN	(517) 377-1746
MINNESOTA	(612) 296-2371
MISSISSIPPI	(601) 965-4346
MISSOURI	(314) 539-2522
MONTANA	(406) 444-4500

NEBRASKA	(402) 221-3281
NEVADA	(702) 885-6396
NEW HAMPSHIRE	(603) 271-3176
NEW JERSEY	(201) 750-9191
NEW MEXICO	(505) 766-2398
NEW YORK	(518) 457-6820
NORTH CAROLINA	(919) 733-7533
NORTH DAKOTA	(701) 239-5415
OHIO	(614) 640-2242
OKLAHOMA	(405) 231-4814
OREGON	(503) 731-4072
PENNSYLVANIA	(717) 787-3687
PUERTO RICO	(809) 754- 5181
RHODE ISLAND	(401) 457-1858
SOUTH CAROLINA	(803) 765-5547
SOUTH DAKOTA	(605) 330-4326
TENNESSEE	(615) 736-5408
TEXAS	(713) 750-1696
UTAH	(801) 524-5700
VERMONT	(802) 828-2157
VIRGINIA	(804) 786-2381
VIRGIN ISLANDS	(809) 773-1300
WASHINGTON	(206) 753-3487
WEST VIRGINIA	(304) 347-5141
WYOMING	(307) 772-2448
WISCONSIN	(608) 266-3133

WHAT CAREERS OFFER APPRENTICESHIP PROGRAMS?

More than 80 percent of all apprentices are in the following occupations. The figures following each career indicate the number of apprentices as of 1990*. This information is from the U.S. Department of Labor.

Electrician	37,033
Carpenter	27,206
Plumber	12,965
Pipe fitter	11,772
Sheet metal worker	11,061
Electrician, maintenance	6, 892
Machinist	6,456
Tool-and-die maker	5, 548
Roofer	5,539
Firefighter	5,281
Bricklayer(construction)	5,058
Cook (hotel and restaurant)	5,007
Structural-steel worker	4,464
Painter	4,349
Operating engineer	3,779
Correction officer	3,636
Maintenance mechanic	3,445
Electronics mechanic	3,310
Automobile mechanic	3,024
Millwright	2,797
Construction-equipment mechanic	2,589
Police officer I	2,512
Airframe and power plant mechanic	2,302
Diesel mechanic	2,228
Electrician, airplane	2,246
Insulation worker	1,815
Welder, combination	1,735
Line maintainer	1,696
Refrigeration mechanic	1,518
Cement mason	1,515
Boilermaker I	1,405

Environmental-control-system installer servicer	1,349
Fire medic	1,325
Line erector	1,317
Cook (any industry)	1,312
Tool maker	1,249
Radio station operator	1,179
Car repairer (railroad)	1,137
Stationary engineer	1,093
Telegraphic-typewriter operator	1,073

*Only apprentices whose registration is recorded on the automated data collection system are counted; these are roughly 70 percent of all apprentices. Data is not included for some States, such as California, and data from other States may be incomplete.

ASK THE RIGHT QUESTIONS

As you examine these apprenticeship programs you may wish to ask some of the same questions that you would ask when you explore colleges, schools, and the military. Your questions should focus on these two things.

1. **"Will this training get my child to his/her chosen goal? Will he/she be able to complete this training?"**

2. **"What are the physical demands of this training?"**
Many of the apprentice programs that we have listed require a great deal of physical stamina. This needs to be taken into consideration.

3. **"What percent of the training will involve classroom training?"**
Some apprenticeships require a significant amount of classroom instruction.

4. **"What does it cost for books and supplies?"**
Most program sponsors provide study materials, but often apprentices must purchase standard manuals. Some apprentices may also be required to provide their own basic tools.

5. **"Does the program offer dual enrollment in a community college?"**
Some programs will allow you to get an associate degree while training.

6. **"Is this apprenticeship program registered with the federal or state government?"**
This question will clarify the quality of the program and will allow you to be sure that the training will be recognized by various employers.

WHERE TO GET WHAT EMPLOYERS WANT

GRADUATE EDUCATION

WHAT IF YOUR CHILD WANTS TO PURSUE A CAREER THAT WILL REQUIRE PROFESSIONAL OR GRADUATE EDUCATION?

Some careers that your child might choose can require more education beyond a four-year degree. Three common choices would be a medical doctor, lawyer, or psychologist. If your child has selected one of these careers, or another career that would require him/her to go on beyond a four-year degree, there are a few extra things that he/she needs to consider.

One the first and most obvious considerations ... is he/she willing to wait more than four years before beginning this career of choice. If his/her desire is strong enough this won't be a problem.

The second and most important consideration ... what he/she will do if he/she doesn't make it all the way. There are two reasons why your child might not make it all the way. First, as students go through their four years of college, some will just get plain tired of it all. Second, admission to graduate and professional schools can be very competitive. Some students won't have the grade point average or standardized test scores to allow them to continue.

PREPARING FOR A BACK-UP CAREER

Because of the possibility that your child might find him/herself in such a position it is best to be prepared. You will basically be preparing a back-up career. The sentence that you would use to fit your choices into would look something like this, "OK, in 6,7, or 8 years I want to be a_____, but just in case I want to stop my education after four years, I will be a _____."

This is extremely important for parents to consider. A lot can happen in the four years that your child is away at college. If, for whatever reason, your child does not go on for that extra education, he/she needs to be prepared to be employable in another career where he/she will be happy and financially independent.

And yes, your child can prepare for that back-up career at the same time that he/she is preparing for professional or graduate school. Many parents are under the false impression that their child has to enroll in a certain "pre" course while attending a four-year undergraduate program (pre-law, pre-med etc.). The truth is that many professional schools will consider students for admission who have majors that are not one of these "pre" majors. These schools do, however, have certain required courses

136

that a student must take before being considered for admission. As long as your child is taking these required courses while he/she is preparing for his/her back-up career your child will be able to choose at the end of three or four years which direction to go---- graduate school or that back-up career.

GETTING WHAT THE GRADUATE SCHOOLS WANT

What you will need to do is get information about the professional or graduate schools that will prepare your child for that primary career choice. You can get this information from the same sources that you used before.

1. A person who is in the primary career that your child has selected. Find out what graduate or professional school they attended or their colleagues attended.

2. Guides in the library or book stores that list all the different schools that offer "post-graduate" (after college) education (look for the same names that appear on the college guides). You will find these books in the same reference sections that you found the Occupational Outlook Handbook and the guides to four-year colleges. These guides will probably have the same publishers so you can contact them as you would have earlier.

3. Your high school guidance counselor may be able to give you some insight based on students that have previously taken this route. Keep in mind, however, that because of the kind of choices that high school counselors are helping their students make, they may not have all the answers to decisions this far out of high school. They will be able to at least give some direction on where else to look.

4. The four-year colleges that prepare students for this kind of school will also be able to tell you what graduate and professional schools are out there.

Now that you know where to look, you need to know what to ask. Start by finding out what the admissions requirements are at these post-graduate institutions. Many post-graduate programs will require certain college courses be taken while getting a college degree and will also require certain standardized test scores. Some may require just any four-year degree and test scores. Whatever the case, determine what those requirements are and keep them handy in the career file that you have created.

GETTING WHAT THE GRADUATE SCHOOLS WANT WHILE PREPARING FOR A BACK-UP CAREER

Once you know the required courses for graduate admission, approach someone at the colleges that your child might be considering. Discuss what course of study your son or daughter can take that will allow him/her to take these required courses and still train for that back-up career. Remember that you are looking for a specific career and not just a subject for your back-up. For example, your son or daughter may want to be a doctor. Perhaps your child could train to be a high school biology teacher or a medical technologist while in college. As long as your child takes the required courses for admission to medical school while training for one of these careers, he/she will be prepared to go on to medical school or enter the job market and be employable after four years. The same approach can be used for students interested in law school and other graduate schools.

Once you have selected this back-up career, and get from the college how they would work-in the courses required by the graduate school, call one or more of those graduate schools. See what they think. If they are confident that this program of study put together by the four-year college of your choice will allow your child to fulfill his/her academic requirements for admission to their graduate program, you are set. If not, go back and make any changes that they recommend.

Turn now to the section of this book on financial aid.

138

PARENT TO PARENT

"(Our oldest daughter) ..took to college like a duck to water- especially the social life. By working at a variety of jobs, she took care of virtually all her living expenses including paying her apartment rental the last two and a half years of college. We paid her tuition and dormitory fees, and the last two years she received low cost loans from a fraternal organization I belonged to. Upon graduation, she moved to Washington, D.C. and went to work for a large lobbying organization. She married the young man she met in college, paid off her loans, and in time presented us with two grandchildren. A couple of years ago she was named Vice President, Finance..."

PAYING FOR YOUR CHILD'S EDUCATION

Can you say stress?

It is now time to go about paying for the educational choice that has been made by your child. This has long been a source of immeasurable anguish for most parents whose child wants to go to school after high school. I have one word for anyone who finds them self in such a dilemma -- RELAX. The financial aid system in this country is designed so that everyone should have the opportunity to go on for higher education despite their income. This is the first reason that you should relax.

The second reason is that just about every college or school in this country is at least partially dependent on tuition in order to pay their bills. And, since they cannot get that tuition unless they have your child as a student, these schools are dependent upon your child. It is with this attitude that I suggest parents approach the financial aid offices at colleges and schools. Don't get me wrong. I am not suggesting that you will have to prepare for battle with the people in the financial aid departments. In fact, you may find that these people will be the most helpful of all the people that you will deal with at the school. The financial aid professionals that I have had the opportunity to work with have been very compassionate people who gain a great deal of reward from helping students overcome their financial hurdles.

Before we go into the procedures that you will need to follow, I want to first go over some of the ways that you will find to pay for school. Most people will find themselves using a combination of many if not all of these sources.

I do want to make sure that everyone understands that I am not a financial aid expert. The information that follows is designed to point you in the right direction. Entire books have been written to help people understand the financial aid process. This is not one of those books. Even if most people read these financial aid books, they probably wouldn't understand everything, and because of changes they might not get the most timely information. The information that follows is designed to give parents an overview and at the very least help parents to understand that their child can afford higher education, one way or another.

142

Grants -- These are lump sum payments given to you by the government or the school to help you pay for school costs. Grants do not have to be paid back. If and how much money you receive in the form of grants will depend solely on need. You will apply for these grants through the school that your child is applying. They will be called **Pell Grants, Supplemental Education Opportunity Grants**(SEOG), and **Institutional Grants**.

Loans -- There are two kinds of loans that are available for helping you pay for school. The first loans are those for which your child will apply. Your child will also be responsible for paying these back. These loans don't require credit ratings and don't require your child to make payments until several months after they graduate or quit their training. There are several kinds of these student loans. You will hear them referred to as **Stafford Loans** (subsidized and unsubsidized), **Perkins Loans**, or **Direct Loans** (subsidized or unsubsidized).

The second kind of loan is one for which the parent will apply. These are called **Plus Loans** or **Plus Direct Loans**. These loans require a credit report on the parents. Parents will begin paying these loans back shortly after their child starts college and payments can be spread out to well after their child graduates.

Work Study -- This is another form of government assistance. If your child qualifies, he/she will work several hours per week for the college in exchange for assistance. Ask the colleges and schools that your child is applying to about these.

Scholarships -- Scholarships, like grants, are funds that do not have to be paid back. There are two forms of scholarships. Need-based scholarships are based on financial need. Merit-based scholarships are given in exchange for your child's academic, athletic, or social achievements. There are also scholarships available for a number of other reasons including association with certain religious, professional, and civic groups. These scholarships are available through your college's financial aid office, the military, and other private organizations.

Part-time employment -- Many students these days face the reality of having to work while in college. There are a number of advantages to this. First, it reduces the amount of money that has to be borrowed. Second, it gives your child an appreciation of the investment that he/she is making. And, third, it allows your child to gain valuable work experience that helps make him/her more marketable. As long as your child's part-time job does not interfere with class or cut into study time, it should be considered.

Savings -- Parents who have had the opportunity to put money away for college will have an advantage. Since a great deal of college costs these days are being covered by loans instead of grants, parents who have put money away in advance will have to borrow less. Your child will also have the opportunity to save during summers and while doing part-time jobs in high school and college. Again, the more they save the less they will have to borrow. One key thing to remember is that savings in the parent's name will decrease financial assistance far less than savings in the child's name. Talk to a financial aid person about when to switch your child's savings over to you name.

Volunteer work -- The National and Community Service Trust Act of 1993 is another way for your child to pay for his/her education. It allows people who are at least 17 to volunteer to do community service work in exchange for college funding. This work can be done while your child is preparing for college or technical school, while he/she is still a student or even after. For information call 1(800) -94-CORPS.

HOW TO GET STARTED

One of the biggest fears that parents have had when it comes to applying for financial aid is that they have to go about this process alone. The fact is, most financial aid officers at colleges and career schools are prepared to walk you through this process. After applying to the schools that your child wants to attend, you will need to ask your admissions officer to arrange a meeting with someone in the financial aid office.

The process of getting financial aid should start early in the senior year. You won't be able to submit forms to the government until January of your child's senior year, but there are a number of things that you will want to do in advance. The first thing that you should do is get a Free Application for Federal Student Aid (FAFSA). This is the form that you will submit to the government in January. This form is used by the government to determine your Expected Family Contribution (EFC). You can get this form at one of the schools that your child is applying to or from your high school guidance office. In most cases this is the only form that you will have to submit. There are some schools that require an additional form called a PROFILE. These will usually be schools that are private and may have significant funds available through the school to give in the form of institutional grants. They use the PROFILE in addition to the FAFSA to calculate your Expected Family Contribution. If one of the schools that your child has selected requires you to fill out a PROFILE, do that immediately in the beginning of his/her senior year. Some schools that require the PROFILE have deadlines in the fall. If you miss that deadline you won't be eligible for these institutional grants. By filling out a PROFILE you may also be given an estimate early of what your financial aid package will be.

When you get your FAFSA, you will see that in order to complete this form you will need certain information, including your latest income tax return, investment and savings statements, as well as information about business assets. Collecting this information now and having it ready will allow you to send your completed FAFSA immediately at the beginning of January. This is something that you want to make sure that you do because some funds have a limit. It's basically a "first come - first served" situation. If you wait until the spring you may be trying to draw water from an empty well. The income tax information that is needed is the information for the year that will end the December of your child's senior year. Because you won't have W-2s for that year, you will be allowed to estimate. Use last year's tax return and your last pay stubs to help you estimate.

You will only need to submit one FAFSA. On that FAFSA you will indicate the schools that your child is considering. The results of this form will be sent directly to those schools.

What this form will do is give the government the information it will use to determine what your Expected Family Contribution (EFC) will be. This will be a dollar amount that you and your child will be expected to pay. You will get this information in the form called a Student Aid Report (SAR). When the schools get your SAR they will then go about putting together a financial aid package that will cover the gap between what the school charges for tuition and your EFC. This difference is called your NEED. The financial aid that you receive to cover this difference will thus be referred to as NEED-based aid. Some schools use this information differently and will come up with amounts that make your EFC at their school higher or lower than at others, but you can expect that the amount of money that you will be responsible for after financial aid will be around the same, in most cases, no matter what the tuition at that school. In some cases there may be larger differences.

If your Expected Family Contribution is higher than the tuition for a particular school your need will be zero. What this means is that the powers-that-be feel that you can afford all of the tuition. You can still receive aid in other forms, but that aid will not be NEED based aid.

So, this is what happens after you submit your FAFSA. If it sounds confusing, don't worry. I have spoken to many parents who have completed this process for their children and still admit that they have no idea what happened. Much of what will happen at this point will be out of your control. All you need to do is make sure that you do the few things that are required of you:

> *Get the FAFSA form
>
> *Get the PROFILE if your college requires it (again, most will not)
>
> *If your school requires a PROFILE complete it immediately at the beginning of your child's senior year and submit it to the school.
>
> * Complete the FAFSA in December.
>
> * Submit your FAFSA to the government address indicated on the FAFSA on January 2.
>
> *Wait several weeks for your SAR.
>
> *Check your SAR to make sure everything is correct.
>
> * Call your schools and ask what your financial aid package looks like.

I suggest you review this with your child's guidance counselor.

FINDING SCHOLARSHIPS

Another thing that you can be doing while you are preparing info for the FAFSA in the fall of your child's senior year is looking for scholarships. As we mentioned earlier scholarships are sums of money that are given to you for education and don't have to be paid back. Most people have the misconception that all scholarship money is only available for students with high academic achievement. Some scholarships will require a certain grade point average or other indicator of academic proficiency, but there are many scholarships that are not connected to academics. There are, for example, scholarships for people who are a certain religion or a certain nationality. Other scholarships exist for students whose parents are in certain professions or work for certain companies. The categories are endless. The only problem with scholarships is that YOU have to find them. There are a number of ways that you can do this.

1) Check on books at your local library or bookstore. There are a number of reference books that will list hundreds of scholarships and where to write to get these scholarships. I've even run across one book that was written by some parents that had found over $300,000 dollars for their children.

The easiest way to go about searching for these scholarships would be to purchase one of these books and keep it at your house. That way you can read the book at your leisure. If you don't want to purchase one of these books, take a Saturday afternoon at the local public library and get the addresses of all the scholarships for which your child may qualify. When you get the addresses for these scholarships you will need to write and get the applications. This approach can take some time but in the long run it can really pay off.

2) Check you place of employment. Many companies and employee associations will have scholarships specifically for their members.

3) Check with the high school guidance counselor. Many community organizations who offer scholarships will notify local

schools of awards that they are giving.

4) Check with computer stores to see if they sell software. There are programs out there available from educational publishers like the College Board that will help you find scholarships. The software package available through the College Board is called the Fund Finder. These packages are nice because they lessen the amount of time that you will spend looking through lists. You can also just enter your personal information and in some cases the computer will spit out the scholarships for which your child will be eligible. Some guidance offices and libraries will have these programs on their computers and will allow you to use them. Some of these programs can be expensive so you might want to check and see if they have any of these programs available for your use in your local high school. You also might want to call the colleges and career schools that your child is applying to and see if they have such programs.

5) If you are familiar with the internet go to

http://www.fastweb.com/

This web site is designed to match your child with any scholarships that he/she might be eligible for. Your child will be required to answer some questions and start his/her own file. The computer will then respond to him/her in his/her "mail box". The service is free and will allow your child to have access to some of the most recent scholarships that become available. There are other sites on the web designed for scholarship searches, but this one is one of the most convenient.

APPLYING FOR THESE SCHOLARSHIPS

I'm sure that some people who are reading this are wondering why, since there is so much scholarship money available, more people don't take advantage of these scholarships. There are two basic reasons;

1) People don't know where to look.
2) Once people find the scholarships, they don't follow through and apply.

Well, now that you know where to look, the follow through is up to you. Go for it. Tell yourself that you will find 10 scholarships, and you will apply for them in September. Setting a deadline and an exact number will serve as motivation.

HANDLING YOUR EXPECTED FAMILY CONTRIBUTION

After your need-based-aid has been determined, you will have to figure out how to cover your Expected Family Contribution. There are a number of ways to do this that will be determined primarily on resources available to you.

If you have money saved, you will obviously look at the possibility of using that money for all or part of your EFC. If you don't have enough money saved, or you do not wish to exhaust all of these funds, you can do a number of other things.

1) Check with the financial aid office and see if there are other loans available that are not need-based. You will find in many cases that these loans are available. They will have the same names as the need-based loans, but will not be subsidized by the government. What that means is that the government won't cover certain interest charges.

For example, if your child takes out an unsubsidized loan the interest won't be deferred until after he/she graduates. If you do take out one of these loans he/she will either need to leave the interest to accumulate or make small monthly payments while still in school. These payments are usually small enough that your child can and should pay them as he/she goes. There will also be parental loans that are unsubsidized. As with any parental loan, a credit report will be required and you will begin making payments while your child is still in school.

Some parents are concerned about their child having to take out loans to pay for education. Sure, nobody wants to have to put their child in debt, but the economic advantages that he/she stands to gain by making this sacrifice will usually far out-weigh the disadvantages. This is just the way it is done now. You would be hard-pressed to find students today that have not had to borrow some money to pay for their education.

Don't feel guilty if you cannot pay for your child's entire education. The days are gone when parents can afford to do this. What you can do is HELP him/her pay for his/her education. What you may wish to do is share with him/her what his/her EFC is and let him/her know that you will pay part of it.

Keep in mind that this is YOUR CHILD'S education. Now that he/she is an adult, there is nothing wrong with expecting him/her to make the same sacrifices that you will have to make. If his/her portion of the EFC is high, reassure him/her that he/she won't have to have this money in-pocket to begin school. The same sources of funding are available to him/her as are available to you.

2) Check with the school where you have applied to see if they will allow you to make monthly payments to cover part of your EFC. You can make part of these payments and your child can pay a part. Again, why shouldn't your child be asked to help make at least part of these payments by working a part-time job. College towns across America are filled with students working in pizza shops and retail stores so that they can help pay for their education. One of the advantages of this, in addition to reducing the amount borrowed, is that your child will get a stronger appreciation of why he/she is going to school. He/she will see that going to school is necessary so that he/she won't have to work at these kinds of jobs for the rest of his/her life.

151

Another advantage of having your child help pay as he/she goes is that he/she will really appreciate the financial sacrifices that are being made on his/her behalf. Realizing what their education will cost will sometimes serve to encourage children to take their studies more seriously.

My only warning to parents is that they make sure that the part-time job that their child takes doesn't take away from study time. Granted, your child will probably spend much less time in the classroom than was spent in high school, but he/she will probably spend that much more time reading, studying, and doing homework.

3) Check with credit unions or banks to see if there are loans available. These will also be loans that have to be paid back while the student is in school.

4) Determine how much your child would be able to contribute by getting a part-time job in the summer. One idea would be to determine how much he/she would have to spend on books and supplies for the next year. Give this figure to your child and tell him/her that he/she will be responsible for saving for this amount in the summer. Or, if you wish to be more generous, tell him/her that he/she will be responsible for paying half. Don't be surprised if he/she finds ways to buy used equipment and books.

OK, there you are. You wanted to know how you were going to pay for your son or daughter's education, and now you do. Well, you at least have an idea of how you are going to do it. The truth of the matter is that every financial aid package is different, and every family will use different approaches to handling their Expected Family Contribution. The important thing is that you and your child realize that you can pay for that education.

One of the most important things that you can remember is to start working with the financial aid folks at the schools you are examining as early in your child's senior year as possible. Follow their lead and you should be fine. Like everything else in this whole process it will be a learning experience.

If you are going through this process now make sure that you put together your To-Do list.

LETS JUST SAY

I hate to bring this next thing up, but I feel that I should at least address this. Let's just say that as going through this process of setting up a way to pay for school you find that you are not in the position to cover your Expected Family Contribution. What do you do then?

Well there are a number of things that you can do.

1. Continue looking at schools that can provide training for your child's chosen career but might be less expensive.

2. Consider looking at your local community college for your son or daughters first year of college. Many students have used community colleges for this very purpose. Make sure that the courses will transfer to the school where your child intends on finishing. The best way to do this is to check directly with the school your child will be transferring to.

3. Return to the books on scholarships and apply for everything and anything for which your son or daughter might qualify.

4. Check into the military. The military can offer significant amounts of money for schooling in exchange for several years of service.

5. Look into any money saving ideas. Living at home and attending a local college can save you the most. In many cases it can save you several thousand dollars per year. Ask the schools if you can purchase used equipment and books. This will save you only a hundred or so dollars, but every little bit helps.

* Whatever you do, keep in touch with the folks at the school that interests your child. Don't ever give up without giving them the chance to do all that they can.

I apologize for having to bring this stuff up after you have been reassured that you should be able to afford your education, but I figured it might benefit you...just in case. I would encourage you to not even think about these things unless you absolutely have to. In most cases you won't.

Keep a positive attitude and go for it! Remember, where there is a will there is a way. If you are like most parents, you will look back at this whole financial aid process and be amazed at how easy it actually was. When you do, make sure that you tell other parents.

I hope that the previous information has been helpful. I feel compelled to remind you that I am no expert on financial aid. The previous information was designed as an overview. For the sake of brevity, I did take the liberty of summarizing. As you go through this process you will be working with people who know all of the intricacies and new developments that may occur. If you wish to have more detailed information there are books available that spell everything out. If you want more information you may wish to contact the U.S. Department of Education. Ask for *The Student Guide to Federal Financial Aid Programs.* The phone number is 1(800) 433-3243.

If you are a working with a daughter or are a member of a minority you may also wish to read *Higher Education Opportunities for Minorities and Women.* It is also published by the U.S. Department of Education. For a copy call (202) 401-3550.

PARENT TO PARENT

"My daughter's selection was textbook - an orderly, decision-tree, shared process that was positively delightful for both of us - and it had none of the turbulence or challenge associated with my son's process. We spoke jointly with her guidance counselor, received direction and suggestions based on the kind of school and environment that best suited her, and even assisted her in the application process when she asked. When we had narrowed the list to 5 schools, we planned campus visits and had wonderful, memorable adventures together. It was a dream - everything I had felt excluded from with my son, my daughter shared with me in spades."

GETTING WHAT
EMPLOYERS WANT

EXPERIENCE

"Been there - done that."

One of the greatest advantages that your child can have when applying for a job is experience. The person who can go to an employer and tell them that he/she has "been there and done that" will be the first person hired. The reason is one of convenience. By hiring someone with experience, the employer will have less "down time" with a new employee. They won't need to take as much time getting a new employee familiar with his/her surroundings and their procedures. The new employee with experience will be able to "hit the ground running" and will be able to be a productive member of that company's work force in a shorter period of time. This is the main reason that employers will ask for experience in the want ads.

Another reason that experienced people can benefit a company is that they can bring in new ideas or unique approaches to solving problems and getting the job done. If I am an employer, and I hire someone who has had some experience with another company, that person might have learned a different set of approaches that when applied to my business might provide a needed boost to production.

Now that you know the value of experience we need to look at some of the opportunities to provide your child the opportunities to get that experience.

WHERE TO GET YOUR CHILD EXPERIENCE

Part-time jobs

Many children will find themselves doing part-time jobs while still in high school. Most will take these part-time jobs in order to have some extra spending cash for recreational activities, to pay car insurance, or to save for their education. In many cases such jobs will be whatever they can find that will pay them a few bucks. So, the idea of working part-time jobs is nothing new. What would be new in this approach is finding part-time employment in a field where they plan to pursue a career. For example if your child wants to pursue a career in the medical field perhaps he/she could approach a local hospital or physician's

158

office.

Obviously the degree of responsibility that your child will be given will be far less than what he/she would be given after formal training, but your child would at least be able to give employers half of what they want when they request experience. In other words your child couldn't tell the employer that he/she has "done that", but your child would be able to tell the employer that he/she has "been there". This kind of experience is still very valuable. By having "been there" your child will able to be comfortable working in this kind of environment and will at least be able to understand how things are to be done.

If your child has the opportunity during high school or during post-high school education to acquire several years of experience, he/she may at that point begin doing some of the very things that their new employer would pay your child to do. This would give your child the second part of the experience ...the "done that".

So when the time comes and your child begins to think about the possibility of getting a part-time job encourage him/her to do so. But, don't let it just be a survival job. Make it a part of the education and assist your child in finding career-related experience.

Volunteering

The world is in desperate need of volunteers. Your child is in desperate need of experience. Put the two together and you have an easy solution to two problems. Beginning in high school, after you have had the opportunity to discuss careers with your child, seek out opportunities for your child to dedicate several hours per week doing free work for an employer or civic association in your area. Again, make sure that you can find opportunities that are closely associated with the career, or at least the career field, where your child has an interest

This is an excellent opportunity for your child to get experience, but is also an opportunity for your child to

159

demonstrate to a future employer that they are in possession of the ever valuable "work ethic". After all, if your child is willing to work for free, certainly he/she will apply themselves when being paid. Volunteering will also prove to a prospective employer that your child is truly interested in working in this particular field. Nothing can be more frustrating to an employer than hiring someone, training that person, and then finding out afterwards that this new employee wants to quit because this is really not what he/she wants to do.

Volunteer work has several advantages over part-time jobs. First -- getting in. It is much easier for a company to bring someone into their organization when they don't have to pay. If your child wants a part-time job with that company, money would have to be found in the budget, and that money might not be there.

Second, you can have more leverage in dictating the schedule. If your child is being paid, the company will need your child for a certain number of hours and at a certain time. By volunteering you can have more say in dictating how much time would be involved and when that time may be.

Third, you can get experience that is customized to your child's experience needs. If you child is hired to work at a company, he/she will have a set job description and will get his/her experience by doing what the employer needs him/her to do. If your child volunteers, you child can say what kind of experience he/she needs and then volunteer in that particular area

If a company in your area does not have an established volunteer program, you may need to help your child with the process. Start by finding someone you know at a company and ask for their help. Get them to steer you to the appropriate departments and contact the people in those departments directly. If you don't know anyone at that particular company contact the personnel department or public relations. Be prepared to sell the idea to them if there is not already a set volunteer program.

Job shadowing.

Job shadowing is something that has been encouraged by the School to Work Initiative. Job shadowing programs are arranged by your local school district and are opportunities for your child to spend time in industry watching a professional in a certain career. We spoke about this earlier when we discussed exploring careers, but it can also be used to allow your child to say "been there".

If you are interested in finding out about job shadowing call your local guidance counselor and ask if he/she has a program that matches your child's interests.

There are advantages to using job shadowing programs. The first one would be that the program is already established. The work will have already been done by people at your child's high school. Another advantage would be that some of the experience is gained on school-time. This can be a motivating factor for getting your child interested.

Internships

Internships are formal programs established by high schools, college's, and career schools. Your child will complete the internship in exchange for credits towards graduation. Some internships will be paid and others will be unpaid, but this should not be your primary concern. The primary concern is that your child will be getting experience.

The School to Work Initiative is responsible for encouraging these internships in the high schools. Some high schools will have these and others will not. To get your child involved with one of these at the high school level you would need to contact your high school guidance counselor and arrange a meeting.

Internships have commonly been available at institutions of higher learning but are not always used. Some schools have recently made internships mandatory. When looking at colleges and career schools make sure that this opportunity is available to your child. Graduating from a college or career school without this experience will put your child in the back of the pack.

A SUMMARY
OF OUR
STEP BY STEP
PROCESS

At this point, it seems appropriate to review some of what has been covered and to give you a summarized overview of the whole process. I will review the points that we covered in chronological order. If you are working with a child that is starting late, try to as many of the early steps as possible or even simultaneously.

CAREER AWARENESS

Remember that it is never too early to begin exposing children to the real world of work. It is critical however that this exposure begins during their early years of high school. Their junior year in high school should be the most important year for career exploration. This will also be the most specific time because they will soon be making decisions that will effect their futures. Use as many of the resources that we spoke about earlier as you can. You must be involved, kids will usually lack the motivation or the sense of urgency needed to do this properly. You are the guide and the motivator.

EMPLOYABILITY SELF AWARENESS

Employability self-awareness is another step that can start very early in high school. Encouraging your child to compare what employers want as far as traits and skills to what he/she already has. The checklist that we covered earlier should be very helpful with this. Remember that as your child becomes more specific with his/her career choices more attention needs to be paid to those traits and skills that relate directly to those particular careers. Using objective people such as teachers to help you child evaluate these traits will be very helpful.

CAREER SELECTION

By the end of your child's junior year in high school, he/she should be prepared to make some choices. He/she may select one career or a few. Encourage him/her to limit his/her choices to the top few. It is time to make decisions. If he/she still can't decide on a career then return to some of the ideas in career exploration. Review his/her choice or choices. Examine each choice to see if it will pass the following test.

1. Does your child feel that this career will be something that they will provide satisfaction?

2. Does the income provided by this type of a career seem to be enough to provide the kind of lifestyle your child wants?

3. Is this career field in demand?

TESTING

Make sure that during your child's junior year in high school he/she has begun taking tests that will be required by colleges and the military. Have him/her take all the tests offered even if he/she feels he/she may not need them. Refusing to take tests like the ASVAB, SAT, or ACTs will close doors to opportunities that might arise. Now is too early to close any doors.

EXPLORING TRAINING OPTIONS

After your child has selected a career, or few careers, it is time to selected "career-appropriate" training. This should be done late in his/her junior year, the summer after his/her junior year, or, at the very latest, early in his/her senior year. Remember that the training option your child examines must be one that will get him/her to his/her career goal. Prepare to use vacation time or weekends to visit various colleges, schools, and other training locations.

APPLYING FOR FINANCIAL AID AND SCHOLARSHIPS

At the beginning of your child's senior year in high school you will need to begin applying for financial aid. If he/she is applying to private schools of any kind he/she will need to acquire a PROFILE and submit that form as early as possible. This would also be a good time to begin applying for scholarships. The FAFSA cannot be sent until the first of January, but you can begin filling out forms. Just leave the information about your income blank until you fill out your tax forms. Many schools can help you estimate your EFC. You can then begin a plan for payment if any is required.

MAKING THE COMMITMENT

In the spring of your child's senior year he/she should have already applied to, and maybe even been accepted to the colleges, schools or other programs that he/she intends to use and be ready to finalize his/her decision on what career will be his/her starting point, what training option he/she will pursue and how he/she will pay for it (if he/she is selecting a school). At this point your child can make the necessary commitments and sign whatever forms need signed.

A TIME TO CELEBRATE

For many students graduation will be more a time of fear than a time of joy. This will not be the case with your child. Instead of heading into the "Great Unknown" as many high school seniors see their future, your child will be heading into a well thought-out, exciting path to success. The question will not be "Is he/she ready for the world?", but "Is the world ready for him/her!"

START CREATING
YOUR CHILD'S
RESUME
NOW

The
"work-in-progress"
resume

Many people wait until after completing their chosen training before putting together a resume. It is a far better idea to begin a resume at the start of training. Not only will it prepare your child to take advantage of opportunities that pop-up during training, it will also serve as a visual reminder of the path that that he/she has chosen. Keep this resume on a word processor or computer. Have your child adjust it every few months to reflect anything new. When printing it out always use the highest quality printer available to you and use a heavy-weight white, gray, or slightly off-white paper.

1. Centered at the top of the resume should be personal information. Your child's name, his/her address and phone number, and an e-mail address if he/she has one.

Joanne Shmoe
111 First Street
Timbucktwo, PA 12345
(123) 456-7890
jShmoe@xyz.com

The phone number should be *his/her* home phone number. Putting the phone number for a dorm room, frat house, or shared barracks phone can result in some embarrassing mishaps. Keep an answering machine on at the number indicated when your child begins to send resumes out. He/she may get only one chance at a position, and he/she wouldn't want to miss it.

2. Below the address should appear your child's career objective. The most common mistake made here is putting a vague statement. The statement "I am looking for an opportunity with a progressive company where I can best use my talents and develop as an employee" just doesn't work any more. Your child will not make this mistake because you have selected a specific training option based on a specific career objective. Keep it very simple.

<u>Objective:</u> To obtain a position as a computer programmer

3.   The next thing that should appear on your child's resume is educational information.   Since this will be early in their career, start with high school information.   List the full name of the high school followed by the school's address.   If your child received any significant awards or had a GPA over 3.0 include this information also.

Follow this information with the information about the current training option that your child has selected. Indicate that your child is still participating in that training.   At the completion of that training you can change the information to indicate completion as well as to list GPA, awards, etc..

When your child has completed his/her training, change the order in which you list the education. For now, put the most recently completed training last.   Usually the most recently completed training will be the one that is most important to prospective employers and needs to be first. You will change the order when your child graduates.
(See examples on the following page)

<u>Education</u>: Timbucktwo High School
           1234 Learning Lane, Timbucktwo, PA 12345
           Graduated May 30, 1999   3.3 GPA

           Podunk University
           2345 Frathouse Lane, Podunk, OH 09876
           Currently seeking Bachelor's Degree in Computer Science
           Will graduate June 37, 2003
                               or

           United States Army
           Fort Rifle
           567 Hup-two-three Avenue, Nowhere,Texas 65432
           Currently training as Information Systems Specialist
           Discharge date - August 23, 2002

4. Following this information should be a section detailing the skills that your child will have when he/she completes the training. This section is where you and your child must really be "sales oriented". Think back to the skills that you were told

would be required in order to obtain your child's desired career. Make sure to indicate here that your child will have these skills. (If in fact your child will have these skills. If you did the previous work in this book you should be on target). Start with the technical skills and follow with the general traits of employability listed earlier in the book. Remember that skills are nouns. These are the *things* that your child "can do".

Skills: Ability to program in FORTRAN, COBAL, and C as well as C++, Smalltalk, Visual Basic, PowerBuilder, and Java

Strong communication and team-working skills

Ability to work without supervision

Obviously, this section will vary greatly depending on the specific position and the applicant. Having this resume saved on a word processor will allow your child to adjust these skills as his/her education continues. Remember that this is a work-in-progress. This resume represents what your child will be when he/she graduates.

5. The selling will continue with this next section. It is now time to detail the experience that your child has had in the field for which he/she is applying and also you child's experience in the world of work in general. As your child progresses through his/her careers he/she will need to drop the "burger shop" jobs and stick with just the jobs that relate to his/her career. For now though, it is necessary to list all of their work experience just to indicate that your child has no "aversion" to work.

Besides the skills section, this can be the most valuable part of a resume. Where the skills section is designed to detail what your child *"can do"*, this section is for detailing what your child *"has done"*. This is where your child can demonstrate that he/she is a proven commodity. List experiences starting with the most recently completed position and ending with your child's first related position or position of responsibility.

Experience:

October 1999- present
> **Computer Lab Assistant**, Podunk University,
> > 2345 Frathouse Lane, Podunk, OH 09876
> coached lab users in proper use of software & hardware
> supervised peer tutoring program for new freshmen

May 1998 - September 1999
> **Clerk**, Goofyboy's Hardware
> > 123 Hammer Lane, Timbucktwo, PA 12345
> ran cash register and assisted in inventory management

On the following page is an example how your child's "work in progress" resume might look as it begins to evolve. Remember to keep it simple and to update it every time your child picks up extra skills, awards, education, or experience.

Joanne Shmoe
111 First Street
Timbucktwo, PA 12345
(123) 456-7890
jShmoe@xyz.com

Objective: To obtain a position as a computer programmer

Education: Timbucktwo High School,
1234 Learning Lane, Timbucktwo, PA 12345
Graduated May 30, 1999   3.3 GPA

Podunk University
2345 Frathouse Lane, Podunk, OH 09876
Currently seeking Bachelor Degree in Computer Science
Will graduate June 37, 2003

Skills: Ability to program in FORTRAN, COBAL, and C as well as
C++, Smalltalk, Visual Basic, PowerBuilder, and Java

Strong communication and team-working skills

Ability to work without supervision

Experience:

October 1999- present
Computer Lab Assistant, Podunk University,
        2345 Frathouse Lane, Podunk, OH 09876
coached lab users in proper use of software & hardware
supervised peer tutoring program for new freshmen
assisted in the development of scheduling software

May 1998 - September 1999
Clerk, Goofyboy's Hardware
        123 Hammer Lane, Timbucktwo, PA 12345
ran cash register and assisted with inventory
management

START
JOB-HUNTING
NOW!

Most people wait until after their training to begin looking for potential employers. Starting at the beginning of one's training can be a major advantage. Not only will it allow a child to be prepared when job opportunities arise, but it can also help to steer some decisions that will need to be made during the training period.

Job hunting can begin as early in this process of career preparation as you would like. In fact, some of what you will need to do may have already been done. In the process of career exploration you may have already begun to collect want-ads and may have spoken to several people in the field. This is some of what you will need to do as you begin this process of job-hunting. Let us next examine some of the things you may wish to do as your child begins his/her training so that he/she will be prepared to go directly training to the world of work.

1. Start collecting want-ads from each Sunday paper.

Now that you know what career your child will be training for, start taking a closer look at each Sunday newspaper that you receive. Look carefully through all of the ads to find your child's career as well as any career that might be closely related.

Most of the jobs that employers are currently looking for in the newspaper will not be around when your child begins looking for careers. However, if an employer is currently looking for the type of training that your child is currently receiving, they will probably still be hiring people with this kind of training when your child begins to look for employment. Keep the names and addresses of all of these employers in a file. You will begin using these companies and other contacts in due time.

Also, keep a close look at the requirements being requested in these ads. As the job markets change, so must your child's training.

2. Build and organize your child's network.

Networking is and has always been one of the best ways to gain employment. By networking, I mean establishing a collection of personal contacts that can be called upon during the time when your child is looking for employment. This process can take some time and might require some phone work, but it will be the most valuable weapon in your child's job-hunting arsenal.

Start by getting a stack of index cards and a small box to

174

contain those index cards. On the top of each index card place the name of one person that you or your child knows. Use one card per name.

Relatives -- Start your cards by using the names of relatives. Leave no one out. Every brother, sister, cousin, nephew, aunt, uncle, grandparent, great grand parent, and second and third cousin, etc. should be listed Even people that you haven't heard from in years need to on your list.

Friends -- Next, begin to list friends. Include your friends, your child's friends, old friends, and even potential friends.

Co-workers & business associates -- The last group that you want on your index cards is business associates and co-workers. This list can continue to grow as you go along. Make it a point to meet new people at your place of work or in your social connections. As you meet new people, put their name on a card. In this case, as you meet new people make note of how you met them and something significant about that person. This can be used to remind someone of the time when you met.

After you have a comprehensive stack of cards, begin listing the phone numbers of these people. Then, list the company and kind of work that these people are involved with. When you are done, each card should look something like what you see below.

Uncle Elmo Smith

(123) 456-7890

Images Incorporated

Corporate advertising

When you have completed this list you may wish to contact these people and ask them if their company hires people with the kind of training that your child is receiving. For each person who says yes or who knows someone who would say yes, highlight the top of their card. This will allow a quick start to your child's search. Remember to keep plenty of extra cards. For each person that tells you, "No, we don't hire these folks at our company, but I know some one who does" make a new card. Staple the new card to the old card so that when your child contacts this referral he/she can inform them of how their name came up.

3. Begin to gather information from organizations and even have your child join professional organizations that are related to your child's chosen profession.

The names of these organizations can be found in the OOH at the end of the section that describes your child's career. These organizations have resources and often provide information about opportunities to their members.

4. Attend Job Fairs.

If you keep an eye on the newspapers of larger metropolitan areas, you will occasionally see advertising for job fairs. These fairs are attended by recruiters from companies who are looking for new employees. While your child is not ready to apply for employment, this is a great way to gather business cards and company contacts that can be used later.

5. Get on the inside.

Many companies like to promote from within. This allows employers to have had an opportunity to "test-drive" a person's performance before making large training and time investments. The trick for your child will to be to get on the inside. There are three main ways to do this. We have covered these earlier in a different context, but they must be addressed here because of their usefulness in job-hunting.

The companies that you wish to get your child into will be those that you have already determined would hire people with your child's training. The positions your child seeks in this process need not be exactly what they are training for, just something that will allow your child to prove him or herself and make contacts.

Part-Time Jobs - It will be advantageous, in more than one way, for your child to be able to secure a part-time job in a company that he/she might like to work for when his/her training has been completed. In this case it matters less what he/she does than that he/she is inside. Even sweeping floors once or twice a week will give your child the opportunity to show that he/she is a hard-worker and dependable. This will also give him/her the opportunity to rub shoulders with the personnel director, department manager's or others who might assist in him/her getting the position he/she desires. Use this approach only while in school or some training. Doing these jobs while attending school or receiving other training will look less curious than if he/she was doing a low-level job after receiving training.

Volunteering - As we mentioned earlier, volunteering to work at a company can be a bit easier than any other approach. While your child will not be receiving pay, college credits, or an organized program of training, he/she will be getting experience and making contacts.

The biggest advantage of volunteering is that your child can request to volunteer in the exact department where he/she may soon be requesting employment. Your child will have the opportunity to associate with the person who may be making the decision about whether or not he/she gets hired. If an opening arises, your child will be the first to know, and may even be in a position to request that the employer hold a position until he/she completes training.

Internships - The most advantageous position for your child to find him or herself in would be the internship. This is a springboard to employment for many job hunters. The training in this case is very comprehensive and involves a great deal more responsibility than the others. This can also the most difficult to set-up. Have your child contact someone at his/her place of education for assistance in acquiring an internship.

As you can see there is a great deal that your child can do

while training to begin the job-hunting process. Please don't allow your child to wait until he/she has finished training.

Nothing can hurt your child more than to be working in a field completely unrelated to his/her training. This raises the eyebrows of an interviewer and could even cost your child the interview in the first place. Your child's first job following his/her training should be one that is related to his/her training and should also be one that allows personal and professional growth. Again, if you follow these directives your child should avoid the pitfalls of having to work outside the field or, worse yet, to not be employed at all for a period of time.

THE
JOB
BLITZ

When your child begins to near the end of his/her training and education it is time to begin the job blitz.

Now that your child is nearing the end of his/her training it is time to put all of his or her preparation to the test. Everything that you have done so far is to about to bear fruit. The one goal will be to achieve the position that your child set as a goal in the very beginning of this process.

I call this a "job blitz" because it will be an all-out assault on the job market. This needs to be a full-time, concentrated effort. You will be presented in the next few pages with some ideas for getting that precious interview. Do not pick and choose. Your child's chance of gaining success will be maximized if you use each of your resources.

1. What about those newspaper ads?

It is now time to dig out all of the newspaper ads that you and your child have been collecting. You will want to send resumes to each of these companies that advertised. Indicate in a cover letter that you remember them advertising at one point for whatever position your child is applying for. Have your child explain in the letter that he/she understands that there may not be a current position available, but that he/she would like to speak to someone about the possibility of a future position. Request in the letter that the person receiving the letter call "at your convenience" soon after receiving the resume. Have them call your home number or a secured phone with an answering machine at a place where your child can be reached.

After a few days, if no one has returned a call, call the employer. Do not hesitate. Many people fear calling a prospective employer because of the fear of turning them off. If the caller is polite and stays brief this should not be a problem. If it does turn out that the person contacted is irritated by the call, they might not be the kind of person that your child would have enjoyed working for anyway.

Push for an interview. Even if a company has no openings (or says they have no openings) ask to visit anyway. This is called an "informational interview". You attend the interview under the guise of finding out about the company, but in some cases it will turn into more. Remind your child that there is only one goal here - TO GET AN INTERVIEW.

When your child is setting up the interview do not let the person he/she is calling set the date and time. This will usually require that person to "check their schedule". While your child has this person on the line, have your child suggest a date and time. Have your child try something like, "I'll be in Yoyotown next Monday.May I stop by in the morning?" This approach takes the pressure out of the decision, and by saying "yes" gives the person that your child has contacted an opportunity to end the phone call and get back to work. More importantly it gets your child an interview.

2. Milk the network

The next step will be to have your child use his/her networking file. Begin with the highlighted contacts - the ones that told you that they knew of a company that hired people with the training your child is completing.

Send resumes to each of these contacts and follow the resume with a phone call. Have your child ask these contacts if they still know of someone who may need his/her expertise. If the answer is favorable, ask for the phone number and address of the contact person at the company. If your contact doesn't mind, have your child request permission to contact this person and have your child ask for permission to use the contact's name. It is most desirable to have your child approach things this way because it allows him or herself to stay in charge. If your child asks the contact to speak to the company, it may be a long time until it gets done. Have your child stay in control as much as possible.

When your child reaches someone at the company that his/her network contact recommended, follow the same approach as describes in the section dealing with want ads.

181

3. Use all your other leads

After completing these first two approaches, your child should call on all the other contacts that have been built in the previous section. Recruiters, professional groups, and any other person or place that hires people with the training your child now has. Use the same approach as before:

> Send resume
> Shortly after, make the phone call
> Ask about openings
> Set a date and time for an interview

This whole process will be the most effective if your child remains pleasantly assertive. Don't allow your child to do this slowly and drag it out. Enthusiasm is a must here. It will be most helpful if you can go through the process of calling and setting up interviews with your child. Make it a game and keep score.

And, by the way, parents should limit their role to guidance and encouragement. Please do not attempt to talk to employers yourself. This can be very counter productive as well as embarrassing. If an employer calls your house, simply take a message and ask when the best time would be for your child to call back.

THE
INTERVIEW
AS A
SALES
PROCESS

**The sale of your child's life. Everyone has got to be a salesperson.
Interviewing is marketing...self-marketing.**

183

Do you want some good news? The hard part is over. The most difficult part of the process is usually acquiring an interview. Once your child has been awarded an interview, the company is, in a sense, saying that they are interested.

While the hard part is over, the process is not. In most cases, if your child is being interviewed so are others. The interview is the opportunity for your child to not only sell him/herself as the right person for the job, but to also convince the interviewers that he/she is also the best person for the job. I will end this book with some tips for making the interview process a success. After this you are on your own.

1. First things first...sell the seller.

As anyone who has ever been in sales will tell you, selling begins with first impressions. It is very important for your child to make the best possible impression when the interviewer first lays eyes on him or her. The following tips will help. Some are industry standards and others are major "snafus" that I have seen while interviewing prospective employees.

A conservative suit. Always have your child wear a conservative suit to the interview. Something with a traditional cut that is made with a quality fabric of black, dark blue, or gray. Please don't have your child wear mini skirts, purple suits, or mom and dad's old dress duds. Invest in an outfit for professional functions only. Dry clean it, and keep it ready in the closet.

A white shirt or blouse. Don't let your child try to be hip in the interview. A classic blouse or shirt, professionally cleaned and pressed, that is white, white, or even whiter is the only way to go. Stay away from patterns and please tell your sons not to wear t-shirts with lettering on them.

A red tie. A safe bet for men is always a red tie. Women should wear a scarf or something that closes the neck of the blouse. Avoid anything with cartoon characters or fish!!!!!

Dark, conservative, clean shoes. No spikes, tennis

shoes, or sandals.

A fresh haircut. Getting a fresh haircut before an interview always helps. The cut should be stylish but professional. Men with pony-tails and women with shaved heads will limit their opportunities. Remember that the interviewer is a person. And, like any other person, can make flash judgments. Don't let your child try to make a social statement during the interview. Your child needs to make one statement - Hire me!

Cleanliness. Believe it or not, some kids have to be told to clean-up for interviews. Have them shower right before leaving for their interview and please have him or her check the nails. I have been turned off on many occasion by a person who has overlooked this. Sorry, but some kids need to be told this, even college grads.

Hey, easy on the smelly stuff. Remind your child to avoid or take it easy on the cologne and perfume. The goal is to impress the interviewer not make them choke to death.

No cigarettes! I cannot count the times that I have been blasted with the smell of a fresh cigarette lingering on the clothes of an interviewee. This can be extremely unpleasant especially on cold days. Whatever your belief is on smoking, if you child smokes, tell him or her not to smoke within two hours of an interview. Thanks.

No inappropriate jewelry. Tabs or jewelry indicating religious, social, or political preferences, or jewelry in ....well....places that look really painful should be avoided.

If your child follows these guidelines, he/she should make it over that first hurdle. As petty as it may seem, it is extremely important.

2. Next step, selling what you have.

After your child has successfully sold him or herself through his or her personal appearance, it is time to begin the

185

real selling.

Have your child try these steps. The interview may vary from time to time, but this approach allows your child to stay in control and to sell like the best salespeople.

Approach the interviewer with good posture, look the person straight in the eye, give a firm handshake and offer an invitation.   (example- Hi, Mrs. Simpson, I'm Icabod Shimbliss...pleased to meet you)

Ask the interviewer what characteristics and skills the company needs for this position. At some point in time, not necessarily immediately, your child will need to ask this question. Good salesmanship requires that you know what the buyer/employer really wants before the selling can begin.

Advise your child to then begin addressing each of the company's needs with a trait or skill that he/she has that will satisfy that particular need. Your child needs to stay focused on those things that the company wants. Your child may have many great traits, but if these traits are not the company's main concerns, your child will waste valuable time. Have your child throw in any other general traits of employability (addressed earlier in the book) only after the interviewer's main concerns have been addressed.

Rehearse with your child the answers to these questions.

1. "What would you say was your greatest achievement?"
2. "What do you think you can offer the company?"
3. "What is your biggest strength?"
4. "What is your biggest weakness?"
   (avoid answering or dwelling on this one)
5. "What do think of your last job?"
6. "What did you think of your last employer?"
   (stay positive)
7. "Where do you see yourself in five years?"

There will be other questions, but these are common. The best overall advice you can give to your child is to stay positive, take a breath to allow thought before answering, and always keep in mind that every answer should be constructed to reinforce that your child is trying to convince the interviewer that your he/she can meet the company's needs. Remind your child to never waste time telling the employer all there is to know. This is not a date. Your child should not be telling - he/she should be selling.

Always tell your child to end the interview with a confident "thank you" and a hand-shake. When your child gets home he/she should send a note of thanks with a few (FEW!) reminder points of what he/she has to offer the employer.

A follow-up call several days later doesn't hurt. If your child gets the job, great ! If not, have him/her keep trying. Victory goes to the persistent job-seeker.

A NOTE TO EDUCATORS

"Sorry, another non-teacher telling you how to teach."

Getting parents armed with the information they will need to help their children become employable is a big step in the right direction. Parents are the key ingredient that has been missing from the process. Now that parents will have the necessary information they should be able to make a huge impact. Nobody, however, can make a larger contribution than teachers. During the school year you are in nearly daily contact with the students in your classroom. Having teachers become actively involved in not just the education of students but also the employability will help greatly.

I know that most teachers are already overburdened with everybody's new ideas about what teachers should be doing. In fact, it seems that a week doesn't go by that someone who has never been in education is telling teachers how to teach. I hope this is not what I am doing. But, if there is some way that you can include career awareness education in your monthly plans, it will help to keep kids focused on careers and career planning.

The reason for including this career awareness education in your classroom has already been stated earlier in the book. There will be many students in your classroom who thoroughly enjoy your class and your subject. Many will even demonstrate a passion for your specific area of specialty. Including some information about careers that relate to what you are teaching might start some of your students on a career path that could reap rewards for them for a lifetime. What an incredible impact you can have on the future of your students.

Including this career awareness in your lesson plans might be easier than you think. Perhaps at your next department meeting you could suggest the idea to the department chair. As a department you could collect enough information and potential speakers to make this a real asset to your students.

Again, sorry for the extra work, but I think it would be a tremendous advantage for your students.

A NOTE TO INDUSTRY

" These are your future employees!"

So far we have focused on the advantages of employability for parents and their children. The advantages to industry are equally as great. I have spoken at several workshops where parents, educators, and members of local industry have come together to discuss making the community stronger through education. At every one of these workshops, the representatives of local companies have expressed frustration at not being able to find qualified employees from the local high schools. This is always a source of friction between the industry reps and the teachers. In one case the entire workshop turned into a disaster, with teachers and industry reps literally yelling at each other.

At this particular workshop one of the industry reps stated that the kids he hires who have just graduated from high school "can't write or do the simplest math functions." This guy was dead meat after that. In response, one of the teachers reminded the industry reps that their best students are going off to colleges and schools. The students that were applying for their positions were in many cases the less motivated students. It was a very good point. Most high school students leave high school to pursue some sort of education or training. Many of the students who are left behind simply aren't prepared to move into the local work force in anything other than menial labor.

This does not have to be the case. In fact if you could design a project to work with the local schools you would not only alleviate some friction, but would also provide yourself with a well trained work force that would be willing to work for a lot less than you might otherwise have.

Let us examine the advantages to your business and how to make these advantages materialize.

As you know, many new business will choose to start in places where there is a large, well trained work force. By going to where the workers are these businesses save huge sums of money. The reasons are very clear.

192

1) Competition. If you have only one person who is qualified to do a certain job in your company, and that person knows it, you had better be prepared to open your wallet. You will be held hostage by a lack of competition. If, on the other hand, you have scores of people with the special skills that you require, the ball is in your court. Not only can you offer less pay, you can also look for other qualities that you might desire for the job.

2) Relocation. Several companies in Ohio recently had to go to Russia to recruit technicians. Certain companies on the west coast are recruiting on the east coast to get enough qualified people to fill the enormous work orders they are generating. In cases like these, companies are paying bonuses, relocation fees, and huge salaries to entice workers to leave their homes and relocate thousands of miles away. Every penny that they use for bringing qualified workers in is a penny out of their profit margins. Hiring local is a lot cheaper than bringing people in.

3) Baggage and bills. Companies that hire college educated or older workers are forced to deal with the baggage and bills brought on by those workers. A person who has borrowed to pay for their education and has had several years to accumulate car payments and credit card bills won't come cheap. These people just won't work for the kind of money that you could pay a worker fresh out of high school. Plus, they may have families and other commitments. This baggage makes them less flexible. Ask anyone with kids if they want to work the midnight shift. The answer will be a resounding, "NO!" Unless of course........the money is right.

So, you can see that having a qualified work force coming from the local high school can be a great advantage. But, how does this get done. The answer is clear. Get together with the local school representatives and let them know exactly the kinds of skills that you will need. Have someone put on paper exactly the kind of training that you need and ask that the information be distributed to the appropriate departments. Volunteer to speak with students to motivate them to focus on these particular skills. Organize a job fair. And, if you are asked to provide internships for the School To Work program, or for any other program, do it. The end result for you will be a lower bottom line, better employees, less on the job training, and a great relationship with the community!

Ideas, comments, suggestions

This book is a work-in-progress. If you have any ideas, questions, suggestions, or personal stories that wish to share, please send them to:

Landon Solutions
309 Lee Drive
Waynesboro, Virginia 22980

Thanks

LOCAL
EMPLOYMENT
INFORMATION

On the following pages you will find a listing of agencies that will give you information on local career opportunities. If they don't have the information, I'm sure they will refer you to an agency that does. You can use this information if your child has expressed a desire to continue to live in the same area as he/she currently lives or if he/she wants to relocate to one of the states listed.

Alabama

Director, Labor Market Information,
Alabama Department of Industrial Relations,
649 Monroe St., Room 422, Montgomery, AL 36130,
Phone: (205) 242-8855

Director,
Alabama Occupational Information Coordinating Committee,
401 Adams Ave., Room 424, P.O. Box 5690,
Montgomery, AL 36103-5690 ,
Phone: (334) 242-2990

Alaska

Chief,
Research and Analysis,
Alaska Department of Labor,
P.O. Box 25501,
Juneau, AK 99802-5501
Phone: (907) 465-6022

Executive Director,
Alaska Department of Labor,
Research and Analysis,
P.O. Box 25501,
Juneau, AK 99802-5501
Phone: (907) 465-4518

American Samoa

Statistical Analyst,
Research and Statistics,
Office of Manpower Resources,
American Samoa Government,
Pago Pago, AS 96799
Phone: (684) 633-5172

Director,
Occupational Information Coordinating Council,
Department of Human Resources,
American Samoa Government,
Pago Pago, AS 96799
Phone:(684) 633-4485

Arizona

Research Administrator,
Department of Economic Security,
P.O. Box 6123, Site Code 733A
Phoenix, AZ 85005
Phone: (602) 542-3871

Executive Director,
Occupational Information Coordinating Council,
P.O.Box 6123,
Site Code 733A,
1789 West Jefferson St., First Floor,
Phoenix, AZ 85005-6123
Phone: (602) 542-3871

Arkansas

Chief,
Arkansas Employment Security Department,
P.O. Box 2981,
Little Rock, AR 72203
Phone: (501) 682-3159

Executive Director,
Occupational Information Coordinating Council,
Arkansas Employment Security Division,
Employment and Training Services,
P.O. Box 2981,
Little Rock, AR 72203-2981
Phone: (501) 682-3159

California

Chief,
Labor Market Information Division,
Employment Development Department,
700 Franklin Blvd., Suite 1100,
Sacramento, CA 94280-0001
Phone: (916) 262-2160

Executive Director,
Occupational Information Coordinating Council,
1116 9th St. Lower Level,
P.O. Box 944222,
Sacramento, CA 94244-2220
Phone: (916) 323-6544

Colorado

Director,
Colorado Department of Labor,
Tower 2, Suite 400,
1515 Arapahoe St.,
Denver, CO 80202-2117
Phone: (303) 620-4977

Director,
Occupational Information Coordinating Council,
State Board Community College,
1391 Speer Blvd., Suite 600,
Denver, CO 80204-2554
Phone: (303) 866-4488

Connecticut

Director of Research, State Labor Department,
200 Folly Brook Blvd.,
Wethersfield, CT 06109
Phone: (203) 566-2120

Executive Director
Occupational Information
Coordinating Council,
Connecticut Department of Education,
25 Industrial Park Rd.,
Middletown, CT 06457-1543
Phone: (203) 638-4042

Delaware

Chief,
Delaware Department of Labor,
University Plaza, Building D, P.O.
Box 9029,
Newark, DE 19714
Phone: (302) 368-6962

Executive Director.
Office of Occupational and Labor Market Information,
University Office Plaza,
P.O. Box 9029,
Newark, DE 19714-9029
Phone: (302) 368-6963

District of Columbia

Chief,
Labor Market Information,
District of Columbia Department of Employment Services, 500 C St.
NW., Room 201,
Washington, DC 20001
Phone: (202) 724-7214

Executive Director,
Occupational Information Coordinating Council,
Department of Employment Services,
500 C St. NW., Room 215,
Washington, DC 20001-2187
Phone: (202) 724-7237

Florida

Chief,
Florida Department of Labor and
Employment Security,
2012 Capitol Circle SE.,
Room 200 Hartman Bldg.,
Tallahassee, FL 32399-0674
Phone: (904) 488-1048

Manager,
Bureau of Labor Market Information-Department of Labor and
Employment Security,
2012 Capitol Circle SE.,
Hartman Bldg., Suite 200,
Tallahassee, FL 32399-0673
Phone: (904) 488-1048

Georgia

Director,
Labor Information Systems, Georgia Department of Labor,
223 Courtland St. NE.,
Atlanta, GA 30303-1751
Phone: (404) 656-3177

Executive Director,
Occupational Information Coordinating Council,
Department of Labor,
148 International Blvd., Sussex Place,
Atlanta, GA 30303-1751
Phone: (404) 656-9639

Guam

Administrator, Department of Labor,
Bureau of Labor Statistics, Government of Guam,
P.O. Box 9970,
Tamuning, GU 96911-9970

Executive Director,
Human Resource Development Agency,
Jay Ease Bldg.,Third Floor,
P.O. Box 2817, Agana, GU 96910-2817
Phone: (671) 646-9341.

Hawaii

Chief,
Department of Labor and Industrial Relations,
830 Punchbowl St.,Rm 304,
Honolulu, HI 96813
Phone: (808) 586-8999

Executive Director,
Occupational Information Coordinating Council,
830 Punchbowl St., Room 315,
Honolulu, HI 96813-5080
Phone: (808) 586-8750

Idaho

Chief, Research and Analysis,
Idaho Department of Employment, 317 Main St.,
Boise, ID 83735
Phone: (208) 334-6169

Director,
Occupational Information Coordinating Council,
Len B. Jordan
Bldg., Room 301, 650 West State St., P.O. Box 83720,
Boise, ID 83720-0095
Phone: (208) 334-3705

Illinois

Director,
Illinois Department of Employment Security,
401 South State St., Suite 215,
Chicago, IL 60605
Phone: (312) 793-2316

203

Executive Director,
Occupational Information Coordinating Council,
217 East Monroe, Suite 203,
Springfield, IL 62706-1147
Phone: (217) 785-0789.

Indiana

Director,
Labor Market Information,
Department of Employment and Training Services,
10 North Senate Ave.,
Indianapolis, IN 46204
Phone:
(317) 232-7460

Executive Director,
Department of Work force Development,
State Occupational Information Coordinating Committee,
Indiana Government Center South,
10 North Senate Ave., Room SE 205,
Indianapolis, IN
46204-2277
Phone: (317) 232-8528

Iowa

Chief,
Iowa Department of Employment Services,
1000 East Grand Ave.,
Des Moines, IA 50319
Phone: (515) 281-8181

Director,
Occupational Information Coordinating Council,
Iowa Department of Economic Development,
200 East Grand Ave.,
Des Moines, IA 50309-1747
Phone: (515) 242-4889

Kansas

Chief,
Labor Market Information,
Kansas Department of Human Resources,
401 Topeka Blvd.,
Topeka, KS 66603-3182
Phone: (913) 296-5058.

Director,
State Occupational Information Coordinating Committee,
401 Topeka Ave.,
Topeka, KS 66603-3182
Phone: (913) 296-2387

Kentucky

Director,
Labor Market Research and Analysis,
Department of Employment Services,
275 East Main St.,
Frankfort, KY 40621
Phone: (502) 564-7976

Information Liaison/Manager,
Occupational Information Coordinating Council
2031 Capital Plaza Tower,
Frankfort, KY 40601
Phone: (502) 564-4258

Louisiana

Director,
Research and Statistics Division,
Department of Employment and Training,
P.O. Box 94094,
Baton Rouge, LA 70804-9094
Phone: (504) 342-3141

Director,
Louisiana Occupational Information Coordinating Committee,
1001 North 23rd,
Baton Rouge, LA 70802
Phone: (504) 342-5149

Maine

Director,
Economic Analysis and Research,
Maine Department of Labor,
P.O. Box 309,
Augusta, ME 04330-0309
Phone: (207) 287-2271

Director, Maine Occupational Information Coordinating Committee,
State House Station 71,
Augusta, ME 04333
Phone: (207) 624-6200

Maryland

Director,
Office of Labor Market Analysis and Information
Department of Labor, Licensing, and Regulations,
1100 North Eutaw St., Room 601,
Baltimore, MD 21201
Phone: (410) 767-2250

Director,
Occupational Information Coordinating Council,
State Department of Employment and Training,
1100 North Eutaw St., Room 103,
Baltimore, MD 21201-2298
Phone: (410) 767-2951

Massachusetts

Director of Research,
Division of Employment Security,
19 Staniford St., 2nd Floor,
Boston, MA 02114
Phone: (617) 626-6556

Director,
Occupational Information Coordinating Council,
Massachusetts Division of Employment Security,
Charles F. Hurley Bldg., 2nd Floor,
Government Center,
Boston, MA 02114
Phone: (617) 727-5718

Michigan

Director,
Bureau of Research and Statistics,
Michigan Employment Security Commission,
7310 Woodward Ave., Room 510,
Detroit, MI 48202
Phone: (313) 876-5904

Executive Coordinator,
Michigan Occupational Information Coordinating Committee,
Victor Office Center, Third Floor,
201 North Washington Square,
Box 30015,
Lansing, MI 48909-7515
Phone: (517) 373-0363

Minnesota

Director,
Research and Statistical Services,
Minnesota Department of Economic Security,
390 North Robert St., 5th Floor,
St. Paul, MN 55101
Phone: (612) 296-6546

Director,
Occupational Information Coordinating Council,
Department of Jobs and Training,
390 North Robert Street,
St. Paul, MN 55101
Phone: (612) 296-2072

Mississippi

Chief,
Labor Market Information Department,
Mississippi Employment Security Commission,
P.O. Box 1699,
Jackson, MS 39215-1699
Phone: (601) 961-7424

Director,
Department of Economic and Community Development,
Labor Assistance Division-State Occupational Information Coordinating
Committee
Office, 301 West Pearl St.,
Jackson, MS 39203-3089
Phone: (601) 949-2240

Missouri

Chief,
Research and Analysis,
Division of Employment Security,
421 East Dunkin St., P.O. Box 59,
Jefferson City, MO 65104-0059
Phone: (314) 751-3591

Director,
Missouri Occupational Information Coordinating Committee,
400 Dix Rd.,
Jefferson City, MO 65109
Phone: (314) 751-3800

208

Montana

Chief,
Research and Analysis,
Department of Labor and Industry,
P.O. Box 1728,
Helena, MT 59624
Phone: (406) 444-2430

Program Manager,
Montana Occupational Information Coordinating Committee,
P.O. Box 1728,
1327 Lockey St., Second Floor,
Helena, MT 59624-1728
Phone: (406) 444-2741

Nebraska

Research Administrator,
Labor Market Information,
Nebraska Department of Labor,
550 South 16th St.,
P.O. Box 94600,
Lincoln, NE 68509
Phone: (402) 471-2600

Administrator,
Nebraska Occupational Information Coordinating Committee,
P.O. Box 94600,
550 South 16th St.,
Lincoln, NE 68509-4600
Phone: (402) 471-9953

Nevada

Chief,
Research and Analysis/LMI,
Nevada Employment Security Division,
500 East 3rd St.,
Carson City, NV 89713-0001
Phone: (702) 687-4550

Director,
Nevada Occupational Information Coordinating Committee,
500 East 3rd St.,
Carson City, NV 89713
Phone: (702) 687-4550

New Hampshire

Director,
Labor Market Information,
New Hampshire Department of
Employment Security,
32 South Main St.,
Concord, NH 03301
Phone: (603) 228-4123

Director,
New Hampshire State Occupational Information
Coordinating Committee,
64B Old Suncook Rd.,
Concord, NH 03301
Phone: (603) 228-3349

New Jersey

Director,
Labor Market and Demographic Research,
New Jersey Department of Labor, CN383,
Trenton, NJ 08625
Phone: (609) 292-0089

Staff Director,
New Jersey Occupational Information Coordinating Committee,
Room 609, Labor and Industry Bldg., CN056,
Trenton, NJ 08625-0056
Phone: (609) 292-2682

210

New Mexico

Chief,
Economic Research and Analysis Bureau,
New Mexico Department of Labor,
P.O. Box 1928,
Albuquerque, NM 87103
Phone: (505) 841-8645

Director,
New Mexico Occupational Information Coordinating Committee
401 Broadway NE., Tiwa Bldg.,
P.O. Box 1928,
Albuquerque, NM 87103-1928
Phone: (505) 841-8455

New York

Director,
Division of Research and Statistics, New York State
Department of Labor,
State Office Building Campus, Bldg. 12, Room 402,
Albany, NY 12240
Phone: (518) 457-6369

Executive Director,
New York Occupational Information Coordinating Committee,
Research and Statistics Division,
State Campus, Bldg. 12, Room 400,
Albany, NY 12240
Phone: (518) 457-6182

North Carolina

Director,
Labor Market Information,
Employment Security Commission of North Carolina,
P.O. Box 25903,
Raleigh, NC 27611
Phone: (919) 733-2936

211

Executive Director,
North Carolina Occupational Information
Coordinating Committee,
700 Wade Avenue,
P.O. Box 25903,
Raleigh, NC 27611
Phone: (919) 733-6700

North Dakota

Director,
Research and Statistics,
Job Service of North Dakota,
P.O. Box 5507,
Bismarck, ND 58502-5507
Phone: (701) 328-2860

Coordinator,
North Dakota State Occupational Information Coordinating Committee,
1720 Burnt Boat Dr., P.O. Box 1537,
Bismarck, ND 58502-1537
Phone: (701) 328-2733

Northern Mariana Islands

Executive Director,
Northern Mariana Islands Occupational Information Coordinating
Committee,
P.O. Box 149,
Saipan, CM 96950-0149
Phone: (670) 234-7394

Ohio

Administrator,
Labor Market Information Division,
Ohio Bureau of Employment Services,
78-80 Chestnut,
Columbus, OH 43215
Phone: (614) 752-9494

212

Director,
Ohio Occupational Information Coordinating Committee,
Ohio Bureau of Employment Services,
P.O. Box 1618,
Columbus, OH 43266-0018
Phone: (614) 466-1109

Oklahoma

Director,
Research Division,
Oklahoma Employment Security Commission,
305 Will Rogers Memorial Office Bldg.,
Oklahoma City, OK 73105
Phone: (405) 557-7265

Executive Director,
Occupational Information Coordinating Council,
Department of Voc/Tech Education,
1500 W. 7th Ave.,
Stillwater, OK 74074-4364
Phone: (405) 743-5198

Oregon

Administrator for Research,
Tax and Analysis, Employment Department,
875 Union St. NE.,
Salem, OR 97311
Phone: (503) 378-5490

Acting Director,
Oregon Occupational Information
Coordinating Committee,
875 Union St. NE.,
Salem, OR 97311-0101
Phone: (503) 378-5490

Pennsylvania

Director,
Bureau of Research and Statistics,
Department of Labor and Industry,
300 Capitol Associates Building, 3rd Floor,
Harrisburg, PA 17120-9969
Phone: (717) 787-3266

Director,
Pennsylvania Department of Labor and Industry
1224 Labor and Industry Bldg.,
7th and Foster,
Harrisburg, PA 17120-0019
Phone: (717) 787-8646

Puerto Rico

Director,
Research and Statistics Division,
Department of Labor and Human Resources,
505 Munoz Rivera Ave., 20th Floor,
Hato Rey, PR 00918
Phone: (809) 754-5385

Director,
Puerto Rico Occupational Information Coordinating Committee,
P.O. Box 366212,
San Juan, PR 00936-6212
Phone: (809) 723-7110

Rhode Island

Administrator,
Labor Market Information,
Rhode Island Department of Employment and Training,
101 Friendship St.,
Providence, RI 02903
Phone: (401) 277-2731

214

Director,
Rhode Island Occupational Information Coordinating Committee,
22 Hayes St., Room 133,
Providence, RI 02908-5092
Phone: (401) 272-0830

South Carolina

Director,
Labor Market Information,
South Carolina Employment Security Commission
P.O. Box 995,
Columbia, SC 29202
Phone: (803) 737-2660

Director,
South Carolina Occupational Information Coordinating Committee,
1550 Gadsden St., P.O. Box 995,
Columbia, SC 29202-0995
Phone: (803) 737-2733

South Dakota

Director,
Labor Information Center, South Dakota Department of Labor,
400 S. Roosevelt,
P.O. Box 4730,
Aberdeen, SD 57402-4730
Phone: (605) 626-2314

Director,
Occupational Information Coordinating Council,
South Dakota Department of Labor,
420 South Roosevelt St.,
P.O. Box 4730,
Aberdeen, SD 57402-4730
Phone: (605) 626-2314

215

Tennessee

Director,
Research and Statistics Division,
Tennessee Department of Employment Security,
500 James Robertson Pkwy.,
11th Floor-Volunteer Plaza,
Nashville, TN 37245-1000
Phone: (615) 741-2284

Executive Director,
Tennessee Occupational Information Coordinating Committee,
500 James Robertson Pkwy.,
11th Floor-Volunteer Plaza,
Nashville, TN 37219-1215
Phone: (615) 741-6451

Texas

Director,
Economic Research and Analysis,
Texas Employment Commission,
15th & Congress Ave., Room 208T,
Austin, TX 78778
Phone: (512) 463-2616

Director,
Texas Occupational Information
Coordinating Committee,
Texas Employment Commission Building,
3520 Executive Center Dr., Suite 205,
Austin, TX 78731-0000
Phone: (512) 502-3750

Utah

Director, LMI & Research,
Utah Department of Employment Security,
P.O. Box 45249,
Salt Lake City, UT 84145-0249
Phone: (801) 536-7425

Executive Director,
Utah Occupational Information Coordinating Committee,
P.O. Box 45249, 140 East 300 South,
Salt Lake City, UT 84145-0249
Phone: (801) 536-7806

Vermont

Director,
Policy and Information,
Vermont Department - Employment Training
P.O. Box 488,
Montpelier, VT 05602
Phone: (802) 828-4135

Director,
Vermont Occupational Information Coordinating Committee,
5 Green Mountain Dr.,
P.O. Box 488,
Montpelier, VT 05601-0488
Phone: (802) 229-0311

Virginia

Director,
Economic Information and Services Division,
Virginia Employment Commission,
P.O. Box 1358,
Richmond, VA 23211
Phone: (804) 786-7496

Executive Director,
Virginia Occupational Information Coordinating Committee,
Virginia Employment Commission,
703 East Main St.,
P.O. Box 1358,
Richmond, VA 23211-1358
Phone: (804) 786-7496

Virgin Islands

Chief,
Bureau of Labor Statistics,
Virgin Islands Department of Labor,
53A and 54B Kronprindsens Gade,
Charlotte Amalie,
St. Thomas, U.S. Virgin Islands 00820
Phone: (809) 776-3700

Coordinator,
Virgin Islands Occupational Information Coordinating Committee,
P.O. Box 3359,
St. Thomas, U.S. Virgin Islands 00801
Phone: (809) 776-3700

Washington

Chief,
Labor and Economic Analysis,
Washington Employment Security Department,
P.O. Box 9046,
Olympia, WA 98507-9046
Phone: (360) 438-4804.

Acting Executive Director,
Washington Occupational Information
Coordinating Committee, c/o Employment Security Department,
P.O. Box 9046,
Olympia, WA 98507-9046
Phone: (206) 438-4803

West Virginia

Assistant Director,
Labor and Economic Research,
Bureau of Employment Programs,
112 California Ave.,
Charleston, WV 25305-0112
Phone: (304) 558-2660

Executive Director,
West Virginia Occupational Information Coordinating Committee,
5088 Washington St.
West, Cross Lanes, WV 25313
Phone: (304) 759-0724

Wisconsin

Director,
Bureau of Labor Market Information,
Department of Industry, Labor, and Human Relations,
P.O. Box 7944,
Madison, WI 53707
Phone: (608) 266-5843

Administrative Director,
Wisconsin Occupational Information Coordinating Council,
Division of Jobs, Employment and Training Services,
201 East Washington Ave., P.O. Box 7972,
Madison, WI 53707-7972
Phone: (608) 266-8012

Wyoming

Manager,
Research and Planning,
Division of Administration, Department of Employment,
P.O. Box 2760,
Casper, WY 82602-2760
Phone: (307) 473-3801

Executive Director,
Wyoming Occupational Information Coordinating Council,
Post Office Box 2760,
100 West Midwest,
Casper, WY 82602-2760
Phone: (307) 265-6715